D0713510

BECAUSE IT IS THERE

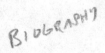

BECAUSE IT IS THERE

Famous Mountaineers: 1840–1940

by

WALTER UNSWORTH

LONDON
VICTOR GOLLANCZ LTD
1968

© Walter Unsworth 1968

575 00083 X

PRINTED IN GREAT BRITAIN
BY EBENEZER BAYLIS AND SON, LTD.
THE TRINITY PRESS, WORCESTER, AND LONDON

CONTENTS

LIST OF ILLUSTRATIONS AND
ACKNOWLEDGMENTS

AUTHOR'S PREFACE

THIS BOOK CONTAINS the brief biographies of some two dozen well-known climbers who helped to found and develop the sport from the early days until the outbreak of the Second World War. Though they are arranged in chronological order they do not represent a comprehensive history of climbing: such an undertaking would need a volume many times the bulk of this one.

The men and women chosen each had something to contribute at various stages of the game. Some, like Whymper, were truly outstanding figures—'all time greats', as the Americans would say—others, by way of contrast, just gave some small but significant mite to the sum total of mountaineering experience. By this choice I hope to show that mountaineering means different things to different people; and give the general reader some idea of the wide and varied appeal of the hills.

The choice of subjects is entirely my own and I am fully aware that there are some significant omissions. Readers who are mountaineers and have their own favourites will doubtless write to me demanding to know why I did not include Moore or Klucker or Willi Welzenbach, or a score of others. That, of course, is the answer—there is at least a score of others.

Mostly I have chosen climbers who are fairly well known by name but whose exploits and backgrounds are seldom found in any detail. In this way, at least, the young tyro struggling up the face of Scafell Pinnacle will know who to blame for Slingsby's Chimney, and the expert having difficulty with the Brenva Face of Mont Blanc can ponder the fact that it was first climbed a century ago.

Two exceptions are Whymper and Mummery, whose careers are fairly well known, especially the former. I felt that they could not be left out because they are such central figures that in one way or another their influence touched on practically everyone else in the book.

The bulk of the book is adapted from a series of articles which first appeared in *The Climber*. They have been altered to make them more easily intelligible to the non-climbing reader, and perhaps they will go a little way towards explaining what it is that makes men climb mountains.

WORSLEY, MANCHESTER   W. UNSWORTH
1968

INTRODUCTION:
CHALLENGE AND CHANGE

NOBODY REALLY KNOWS when men began climbing mountains for reasons other than economic necessity or military advantage, though mountaineering historians, anxious to fix a date, have put forward several various isolated instances of endeavour. All that these prove, really, is that the lure and challenge of the peaks and precipices have stirred the human mind from the days of antiquity.

But this strange fascination which mountains have over a great many people, amounting almost to 'mountain fever', is a fairly modern thing when taken in the mass. Man's primary concern is with food and clothing and finding a roof for his family, and until a state is reached where these are readily available he has not time for the finer points of life. This is why mountain climbing is most popular in highly civilized countries and it is also why it was virtually unknown until the middle of the last century.

Of course easier communications helped and the spread of the railway probably did as much as anything to make climbing possible, but basically it was a phenomenon directly related to wealth and leisure. England was at that time the wealthiest country in the world, thanks to the rapid growth of manufacture and her overseas trade, and so the majority of the pioneer climbers were British, though not all of them, by any means. Naturally only certain classes of society were affected; those with sufficient wealth and leisure to afford six weeks in the Alps, principally the prosperous upper middle classes: manufacturers like the Wills family of tobacco fame, the Pilkingtons with their coal mines and glass works, together with professional men of church, law, university and science.

What was it that prompted these men to risk their lives and suffer extreme discomfort, when they could just as easily have stayed comfortably in their elegant mansions or lorded it at Biarritz? I think the answer is all tied up with the age in which they lived, particularly since the Victorians were great seekers after factual knowledge, and the realization that the world was an unknown oyster which they were on the point of prising wide open. Great explorers like Livingstone and Stanley were making fantastic discoveries in Africa, slowly but inexorably the plains of America were being rolled back, and everywhere daring men were going further, longer, deeper or higher than men had ever been before. Suddenly, in this climate of discovery, men found in Europe, on their own doorstep as it were, a vast region as completely unknown as the Dark Continent— the Alps.

And so in its infancy at any rate, mountain climbing was a product of discovery. The challenge was simply one of going where nobody else had been, just to see what it was like.

But the Victorian age was also an age of Science and though mere discovery was enough for some, there soon followed men such as Professor John Tyndall who saw in the Alps a new region of study, especially the remarkable glaciers about which so little was then known. Tyndall was a true scientist, a professional, but much of the 'science' associated with those early days of climbing was conducted by amateurs, often merely as an excuse for climbing—many people thought the early alpinists quite mad, and 'science' in one disguise or another frequently provided a good excuse to try and make the climbers look 'respectable'.

Nevertheless, the Alps were so new that there was room for all sorts of pioneering work. Exploration of the remote valleys and the high passes was quite as rewarding as the actual conquest of new summits. Discovery, whether scientific or topographical, was the keynote of the era.

Perhaps the greatest discovery that the early pioneers made was that in every Alpine village there existed men with a considerable fund of local knowledge and mountain expertise. These men they hired as guides and porters to carry their luggage and though for the most part they were nothing more than 'pointers of paths' as Whymper so sarcastically put it, and frequently dishonest by all accounts, a nucleus of them rapidly became expert mountaineers whose services were avidly sought after by the climbers.

Without the guides climbing might have been set back a quarter of a century—or it might more rapidly have become the sort of sport it largely is today. It is pointless to speculate but it can be said with certainty that the foundations of Alpine climbing rest upon the combination of the daring amateur and skilful guide of those early years. Perhaps the greatest of these guides were Christian Almer, Melchior Anderegg and Michel Croz, but there were others, too, principally from Chamonix and Grindelwald, scarcely less enterprising. They founded a tradition of skill and service upon which the present day highly organized guides' associations are formed.

Though discovery was the keynote of the early ascents, conquest—the actual satisfaction of overcoming difficulty—was always mingled in with it. At first it took the form of climbing the highest mountains, on the simple plan that the biggest must be best, though in fact this turned out untrue. Most of the really big Alpine mountains have a relatively easy way up and any difficulties are those of conditions and weather rather than technical problems. Nevertheless mountains like the Dent Blanche, the Aiguille Verte and La Meije were notable achievements.

The crux came with the ascent of the Matterhorn in 1865 and it really is quite remarkable how this mountain has dominated Alpine achievement at almost every period from the Golden Age until the present day.

Whymper's ascent of the Matterhorn was not motivated by discovery at all but by a pure desire for conquest—he wanted to be the first to the top and was willing to go to almost any lengths to achieve that aim. This fanaticism was something new —but it brought rewards: not only did he climb the Matterhorn but he made a great number of other first ascents as well.

Whymper did not care in the least how he got up the Matterhorn so long as he was first to the top, but in that same year

Mathews, Moore and the Walkers, led by the Andereggs made the first ascent of Mont Blanc by the Brenva Ridge—a considerable achievement. Here the conquest was not of the mountain top—Mont Blanc had been climbed hundreds of times—but of the steep Brenva Face itself. The challenge was changing. The route was beginning to matter as much as the summit and from that time onwards the development of Alpine climbing has been the ever-increasing importance of the route and its technical difficulties.

Of course, there were still plenty of untrodden summits still to be found, but with one or two exceptions these were what the old pioneers regarded as minor peaks and therefore not worth bothering with. Whymper, for example, climbed the Verte, but he would never have considered climbing the Drus or the Grépon which are considerably lower. In fact, though these splendid spires dominate much of the Chamonix scene Whymper never even *mentions* them in his book.

It was even rumoured amongst the older climbers that when all the large peaks had been climbed there would be nothing left to do and the Alpine Club would wither away and die. They still saw the sport in terms of exploration and sheer height but the new climbers who were emerging saw something quite different. They saw technical difficulty in the smaller peaks and in new routes on the larger mountains.

Rock climbing became more of a skill because it was necessary to be a competent rock climber to get up the new routes. A man may climb Mont Blanc simply by putting one foot in front of the other for a few hours and hiring a guide who knows the way, but such pedestrian tactics will not get anyone to the top of the Drus nor will it get him up Mont Blanc by the Brenva Face routes, no matter how good his guide. Technical ability is required.

Guiding, too, began to undergo a change. The great majority of guides were not technical experts and in any case they saw their craft simply as a dangerous but well paid job (by local standards that is). Consequently in places like Chamonix and Zermatt the tendency was to stick to the regular expeditions

like Mont Blanc and Monte Rosa where they knew every step
of the way and the risks were minimal. There were exceptions,
naturally, but it was mostly from new centres that a fresh kind
of guide began to appear, centres like the Saas valley and the
Bregaglia, where the peaks were rocky and rock climbing
seemed inbred in the natives. Burgener, Venetz, Imseng,
Klucker, Rey—these were the men who now teemed up with
the leading amateurs to push the limit of difficulty far ahead of
what it had been.

Between them they climbed the rocky spires and the long
rock ridges which were the current challenge, and surprisingly
enough, they proved to be excellent ice climbers too. Imseng's
great lead of the Marinelli Couloir on Monte Rosa in 1872 and
Burgener's ascent of the Col du Lion, showed that skill on ice
and snow was not dormant.

This period—the 1870's to 1890's—has often been called The
Silver Age to distinguish it from the Golden Age of the legend-
ary pioneers. In many ways it is the most fascinating period of
all because it corresponds more nearly to our own modern con-
ception of the sport. It gave rise to a whole galaxy of heroes,
though at the time they themselves would have been surprised,
to say the least, to be so described. To name them all would fill
several pages, but many appear in this book; they are the men
to whom modern climbing owes most.

The dominating figure was, of course, Mummery, who
teamed up first with Burgener and Venetz and later on with
Slingsby, Hastings and Collie. The Zmutt arête of the Matterhorn, the ascent of the Charmoz and Grépon, the Teufelsgrat
on the Täschhorn were notable climbs, though Mummery's
spectacular failures—the Furggen ridge of the Matterhorn and
the north face of the Plan, were just as important in their own
way. Mummery was the first of many famous climbers to perish
in the Himalaya.

It was during the Silver Age, too, that climbing began to
gain stature as a subject for writers, historians, painters, photographers and even technicians. The Rev. W. A. B. Coolidge,
who made more ascents than any other man, including some

important ones, became the sport's historian supreme. As an Alpine authority he has never been excelled.

In Britain, rock-climbing as an end in itself, rather than as a way up a mountain, began to attract a small group—Haskett Smith climbed Napes Needle on Great Gable in 1886 and about the same time Puttrell was making the first gritstone climbs at Wharncliffe, near Sheffield. Many of the best Alpinists were also leading rock-climbers at home: Slingsby, Collie, Solly and others, though not Mummery or Coolidge who both thought very little of British climbing. Just as in the Alps, there were ascents which were well ahead of their time—Eagle's Nest Ridge on Gable, Botterill's Slab on Scafell and the Ben Nuis Chimney in Arran could be quoted as examples of this.

By the turn of the century it is fair to say that the original motivation for climbing, discovery, had vanished completely except in remote parts like the Himalaya where exploration was very real. The Himalayan story, however, was still in its infancy and there were no techniques yet evolved to compare with the developments at home and in the Alps.

For the brief period before the First World War climbing continued along the traditional lines but with ever-increasing difficulty as the easier or more obvious routes were ticked off. In Britain Herford and his friends made the first ascent of Scafell's Central Buttress in 1914; a climb which maintained its reputation as the hardest in the country for many years. In the Alps climbers like Ryan and Young, together with Continental experts were putting up sensational new climbs of extreme difficulty, aided by guides like the Lochmatters and Knubel.

But the spirit of Mummery was dying, or at least, becoming ossified. A sort of hallowed tradition was growing which stunted natural growth, tending to turn the sport in on itself. Anything new was looked on with disfavour, even such logical devices as crampons and short axes: pitons were devillish foreign inventions alien to the British way of life.

The pioneers themselves had none of this cant; they made their own methods, unfettered by public opinion. In Britain at

THE MATTERHORN · For over a century this mountain has offered more 'last great challenges' than any other. From left to right can be seen the Furggen, Hörnli and Zmutt ridges. The north face lies between the last two. In the background, right, is the Dent d'Héréns.

LA MEIJE · The last of the great Alpine peaks to be climbed.

THE CHAMONIX AIGUILLES · From left to right, the Charmoz, Blaitière and Plan groups. The glacier of the Plan North Face can be easily seen.

least, such freedom was not won again until after the Second World War.

But by now the climbing was what mattered: the pure joy of moving safely on difficult rock or ice, confident in one's technique and companions. For ninety per cent of climbers this is still the chief attraction of the sport.

The First World War brought many changes, not least in attitude. The leading climbers began to exploit the great faces, following the lead given them by Young before the war, and one by one the last of the famous ridges which had defied attack began to succumb—the Mittelegi on the Eiger, the Peuterey and Innominata on Mont Blanc, the Aiguilles du Diable, the north ridge of the Dent Blanche and others of similar length and difficulty. In a way this was traditional and logical, but on the faces of the mountains new dangers were accepted by risking avalanche and stonefall, at least in parts—Smythe and Graham Brown climbed the Red Sentinal and the Route Major on Mont Blanc and Hans Lauper began his brilliant Oberland campaign which culminated in the Lauper Route of the Eiger.

From the Eastern Alps a new wave of daring climbers known as 'the Munich School' began to attack faces which were not only long and difficult but highly dangerous as well. Most, but not all, of these faces were turned to the north and *nordwand* climbing became the ultimate expression of mountain faith or folly, depending on one's viewpoint. The Schmid's ascent of the Matterhorn north face in 1931 was the first really big break-through of a period which reached a climax in the ascent of the Eiger north wall in 1938. Many good climbers died in these attempts, especially on the Eiger, and at the time the whole creed of north wall climbing was attributed to political fanaticism on the part of fascist youth.

In reality it was once again the challenge which was changing. After all, if a man reaches such a pitch of expertise that he can do everything that has been done previously, and knows he can do it, then any challenge it might once have had, vanishes. Such men can only seek new challenges, or there will be no progress.

2

For those who rejected the alpine north faces as unjustifiable, the greatest challenge lay in the far away peaks of the Himalaya. Everest dominated the era, as far as the British were concerned, and what at the outset had seemed a fairly easy climb turned into a war of attrition as expedition after expedition failed to reach the top.

The British did very well in the Himalaya during this period between the wars, especially with small teams. The most notable were those of Shipton and Tilman—the forcing of the Rishi Ganga, an almost impenetrable gorge, and the subsequent ascent of Nanda Devi being especially striking.

At home the rock climbers were steadily pushing up the standards of the highest climbs but here, more than elsewhere, achievement was closely bound up with the leading personalities such as Longland, Kelly, Kirkus, Edwards and so on—the great bulk of climbing was of a much lower standard.

And so, by the outbreak of the Second World War, climbing had already undergone many changes since it was first conceived. In the following pages you can read the lives of some of those who met each challenge as it came, and those who helped to change the challenge as the years went by.

THE CLIMBERS

ALBERT SMITH

(1816 – 1860)

THE NINETEENTH CENTURY was an age of great showmen.
It was a time when entertaining, forceful and flamboyant personalities paraded the exhibition halls and theatres of the civilized world amazing the newly educated middle classes with
wonders they never knew existed. Barnum and Baily stormed
the circus world, Annie Oakley and Buffalo Bill Cody created
a legend out of the American West, and Edward Whymper
made the Matterhorn the best known mountain in the
world.

And in a way, the great surge of adventure which led to the
conquest of the Alps, had its beginnings in the brash atmosphere
of popular entertainment. Albert Smith was a showman in the
classic mould. Coming twenty years before Whymper, he was
not really a mountaineer at all, and yet, paradoxically, it was
he who helped to start it all.

Smith was born of middle class parents in Chertsey in the
year 1816. At the age of 10 he was given a book called *The
Peasants of Chamouni* in which he read of the tragic ascent of
Mont Blanc made by Dr. Hamel's party in 1820 when the three
of the party were killed by an avalanche in what was the first
great Alpine accident. The story fired the boy's imagination
and was reinforced by reading De Saussure, Auldjo and other
early Alpine writers.

From that time on Mont Blanc became an obsession with
Smith and he determined to reach the summit.

It was many years before he could fulfil his ambition but it
is as well to be quite clear what that ambition was. Smith was
not trying to make a first ascent of the mountain—that had been
done in 1786 by Balmat and Paccard—nor was he trying for the
second or third ascent. In fact a number of people had reached

the top before him, including women. All Smith wanted to do
was simply climb the mountain for his own satisfaction.

In 1838, when he was a medical student in Paris, Smith
begged a lift to Chamonix and was rewarded with his first sight
of the mountain which dominated his thinking. He could not
afford to climb it as a tourist—the cost was considerable as we
shall see later—but he was so determined to get up that he tried
to hire himself out as a porter, though without success.

He soon quit his medical studies and tried to earn a living as
a writer. In this he was modestly successful—he adapted some
plays and his work appeared in leading journals such as *Punch*
and the *Illustrated London News*, but he was far from achieving
fame and fortune. From time to time he visited friends in
Chamonix, though he never had enough money to attempt
Mont Blanc.

The real turning point came in 1849, when, after he read
John Auldjo's account of Constantinople and the Nile, he
managed to visit both of those places. In those days the East was
an area of mystery and when Smith came home he found plenty
of people anxious to listen to his tales of travel.

Now it so happens that some years before he went to Egypt
Smith and his brother had toured outer London giving lectures,
about Chamonix and glaciers, which were quite successful. The
idea of turning his Eastern travels into a sort of illustrated lecture on a lavish scale, now occurred to him. He called it *The
Overland Mail* and it was enormously popular. For the first time
in his life, Smith was in the money!

Two years later, happily prosperous from the proceeds of his
show, Albert Smith set out to conquer Mont Blanc.

In Chamonix he met three companions for the adventure:
Francis Philips, the Hon. W. E. Sackville-West, and C. G.
Floyd. Nothing was left to chance: by the time they started,
being delayed a day by bad weather, they were one of the most
sumptuously equipped expeditions to leave the valley.

The four principals led the way with Smith himself hand-
somely accoutred for the ascent, wearing high leggings tied
with scarlet garters, Scotch plaid trousers, a helmet of best

worsted, a green veil and blue spectacles. Then came sixteen guides and behind them about twenty porters, scroungers and general hangers-on. The enormous provisions included forty-six assorted fowls and ninety-six bottles of wine. It cost Smith and his friends £285, which was a considerable sum in those days.

In view of the expense Smith might have been granted some little excitement to liven the tedious plod to the top, but in fact the whole ascent went off without incident. In his own description, however, he said that he staggered and reeled on the terrible glaciers, falling down utterly exhausted once the summit was reached. This is hardly surprising in view of the fact that there was only one bottle of wine left!

The descent was a hilarious affair. Everyone chose his own route down—some glissaded, some slid, and some, just for the fun of it, rolled down sideways! The remarkable thing is that everyone reached the Pavillion des Pèlerins safely, where they consumed a couple of dozen more bottles of wine before returning to Chamonix. Their reception was tremendous: guns fired salutes, musicians played, little girls presented bouquets and Chamonix had a field day.

Alas for poor Smith! The excitement (or the wine) was too much for him. He had nightmares all night and a raging thirst which made him drink the entire contents of a large water jug before the morning.

On his return to England, Smith wrote *The Story of Mont Blanc*, which he first had published privately but which subsequently ran to many editions. He also mounted another show at the Egyptian Hall, Piccadilly, describing his ascent and illustrating the talk with clever, if somewhat dramatic, backcloths.

The Ascent of Mont Blanc was a winner from the start. Smith caught the public's fancy and the show ran for six years, had three Royal Command Performances, and made £30,000. Indeed, as Whymper dryly commented, had it not been for Smith's untimely death it might have been running yet!

Smith became an overnight celebrity, the 'Mont Blanc Man'. Someone invented 'The Game of Mont Blanc' (rather like

Snakes and Ladders) and orchestras played 'The Mont Blanc Quadrille' and the 'Chamonix Polka' at all the fashionable balls.

But success brings penalties as well as rewards, and whether through jealousy or because Smith was something of a dandy in the way he dressed, he was not much liked by his contemporaries. One man said that Albert Smith's initials were only two-thirds of the truth about him, and Charles Dickens resigned from the Garrick Club when Smith was elected a member. Yet all the evidence seems to suggest that Smith was really a kindly man of cheery good nature.

Smith retained his interest in the mountain which had brought him fame. He gathered together a number of people who had climbed Mont Blanc and almost succeeded in forming a club, but it came to nothing. It would have been the first 'Alpine' club and in fact, Smith did join *the* Alpine Club when it was formed in 1857.

He died in 1860, a wealthy man. His entertainment had been watched by thousands of people, and especially young people, and they had been enthralled. Chamonix and the Alps had been brought home to the phlegmatic British as never before. It caught and fired their imagination. The result was called The Golden Age of Alpine climbing.

THE WALKER FAMILY

Francis Walker (1808 – 1872)
Horace Walker (1838 – 1908)
Lucy Walker (1835 – 1916)

ONE OF THE most remarkable features about the early days of mountaineering is the way in which it was so often a family affair. Whole families went out for the long Alpine season, and whilst Momma and the girls occupied themselves at Bel Alp or the Riffel, the men went out and climbed mountains. Sometimes, however, the girls climbed too.

Of all these family groups, one of the best known is that of the Walkers from Liverpool. Not only did the father and son between them span the entire Golden and Silver ages of Alpine climbing, but Lucy Walker was one of the first women to take up serious mountaineering.

Frank Walker was a prosperous lead merchant with premises in both Liverpool and Chester. He was educated at Charterhouse and then at Pestalozzi's famous school at Yverdon in Switzerland. Whether Pestalozzi's enlightened methods of education turned the boy's head towards the wonder of the hills there is no means of knowing, but at the age of 17 he crossed both the Théodule Pass and the Oberaarjoch.

These youthful ascents must have remained in his memory through his early working life and he probably spoke of them to his son Horace. That young man, in turn, climbed the Vélan at the age of 16—the first of many climbs extending over the next fifty-two years.

In 1858 the family assembled at Zermatt and began to climb together as a party, though the father had not climbed anything for thirty years, the son had made only one ascent and the daughter, so far as we know, had never set foot on a mountain. They began modestly enough—the Théodule Pass and the even

2*

easier Monte Moro Pass. These were not startling achievements, but it was considered very daring for Lucy to take part.
It was the start of a climbing career that was to include ninety-
eight ascents, including most of the principal peaks—on only
three occasions did she fail to reach the top.

Victorian lady climbers had to contend with much more than
the mountains, of course. They had to fight prejudice against
their sex, and they had to climb in clothes which were acceptable to society though very inconvenient on a mountain. Lucy
Walker, for example, climbed in a white printed frock of ankle
length which she used to smooth most meticulously before she
returned to the hotel after an expedition.

Perhaps what puzzled most people who knew about her
mountain climbing was the fact that Lucy was not at all the
hearty outdoor type who rode to hounds with the County. Her
only other exercise was croquet, which is hardly good training
for the Alps, and in every other respect she was the perfect
example of Victorian maidenhood—keen on social work, a
vivacious hostess, good needlewoman, and conversant in several
languages.

Her portrait appears in Whymper's famous engraving of
The Club Room at Zermatt in 1864. Her face had a strong Gaelic
cast for she was Scots on her mother's side, which might explain
her forthright manner of speech and her iron will power.
Undoubtedly it was this inbred determination which helped
her to succeed as a mountaineer.

All of Lucy's climbs were done with her brother or her father
and they had the services of Melchior and Jacob Anderegg of
Meiringen, cousins, and two of the best guides of the day. The
Andereggs, in fact, became more like friends than mere guides,
and Big Melchior, as he was called, always addressed Frank
Walker as 'Papa'. Even when her climbing days were over
Lucy never failed to make an annual visit to the Anderegg
chalet near Meiringen.

Horace Walker was with Whymper and Moore during their
famous Dauphiné campaign of 1864, taking part in the first
ascent of Les Ecrins. Though he never climbed with Whymper

again, he became a close friend of Moore, and the two men were constant companions until the latter's death in 1887.

After leaving Whymper, Horace joined his father and sister to make an ascent of the Grand Combin, the Aletchhorn, the Eiger (fourth ascent) and the first ascent of the Balmhorn. The Balmhorn is not a particularly difficult mountain, but this was probably the first occasion a woman had taken part in a major first ascent.

In the following year Frank Walker and his daughter crossed the fearsome Moming Pass—the first to do so after Whymper—then made their way by the Breithorn into the Aosta valley. They climbed Grivola, and then Lucy was left behind whilst Frank joined his son, Moore and G. S. Mathews for an attack on the Brenva Face of Mont Blanc.

The southern aspect of Mont Blanc is not at all like the dome-shaped front which the mountain presents to Chamonix. Instead it takes the form of an immense, precipitous face complicated by huge ridges and gullies. One part of this great complex overhangs the Brenva Glacier and seems to offer a direct, if steep, way to the summit. This is what the Walkers attempted in 1865.

Led by the two Andereggs they climbed up a spur of the vast face and came upon a knife-edge of ice. This was so exposed that they crossed it by sitting astride, as on a horse, and were able to look down countless hundreds of feet on either hand. Beyond the ice ridge the main face reared up, barred with a line of ice cliffs which it took all the skill of the Andereggs to overcome. When they finally reached the top of the mountain it was with much relief—they had been near the limit of their powers and they knew it.

It was, in fact, a tremendous achievement for the time, and even today ranks as a difficult expedition suitable only for experts. Equally remarkable is the fact that Frank Walker was already 57 years of age at the time!

For his son Horace, the Brenva Face was the climax to a season loaded with achievement. With Moore he had already made the first ascent of Piz Roseg, Pigne d'Arolla, and Ober

Gabelhorn, as well as opening up several new passes across high cols.

About this time too, Walker and Moore, along with Kennedy and other hardy spirits tried their hands at winter climbing in the Alps, and though they did not achieve anything spectacular it was the start of a new idea in climbing which was to mature over the years.

In 1868 Horace reached the highest point of the Grande Jorasses, that magnificent mountain near Mont Blanc which Whymper had climbed three years previously. Whymper, however, had not gone to the true summit, contenting himself with a slightly inferior one now called the Pointe Whymper. Walker continued along the craggy crest of the mountain to what is now called the Pointe Walker—made famous in recent years by the climbs done on its great north ridge, the Walker Spur.

Three years later, in 1871, came the ascent of the Matterhorn by Lucy Walker and her father. It was the nineteenth ascent of the mountain but the first by a woman and almost certainly the first by anyone as old as her father, who was 63 and already a dying man with an incurable disease.

When the news of this expedition reached England Lucy was the subject of an amusing, though not unkind, verse in the magazine *Punch*.

Unfortunately Horace missed the Matterhorn climb because he was nursing a broken arm at the time and his customary place was taken by a friend of the family, Frederick Gardiner, who was also a good climber. It proved to be many years before Horace climbed the Matterhorn—'my bugbear', he called it— and it was a constant source of embarrassment to him. Whenever he was introduced to non-climbers almost the first question they asked was 'Have you climbed the Matterhorn?' And when he confessed that he had not, their opinion of him slumped badly. Even today this attitude is not uncommon—nobody will believe you are an alpinist unless you have climbed the Matterhorn! Quite recently a well known British climber went up the peak solo, and when I asked him why he had bothered with what to him was an easy climb he replied, 'To get the damn thing out of the way!'

Frank Walker died in the year following his Matterhorn climb and for a number of years Lucy continued to climb with her brother, though eventually she too gave up and confined herself to long valley walks, often with her life-long companion, Melchior Anderegg.

Her brother's career, however, continued for many years. In 1874 he went to the Caucasus with Moore, Grove and Gardiner where they made the first ascent of Elbruz, the highest mountain in Europe.

After Moore's death in 1887, Horace Walker joined his friends the Pilkingtons, and it was with Charles Pilkington that he made the last of his 'first ascents'—that of the west ridge of the Dent Jaune in the Dents du Midi. He did not give up climbing, though—his long record shows numerous first class ascents including that of the Charmoz in 1892, then still regarded as one of the more difficult Chamonix aiguilles. He took enthusiastically to the new wave of guideless climbing which came into vogue about this time and the newly discovered climbing in the Lake District. He was particularly active in Skye where he made the first ascent of Sgurr MhicChoinnich, Clach Glas and Sgurr na h-Uamha.

From 1890 to 1892 he was President of the Alpine Club, an honour which few deserved better than he. His last Alpine climb was in 1905 when he was 67, and he chose the snowy dome of Pollux near Zermatt—the only big mountain in the district which he had never climbed before.

Horace Walker died in 1908, his sister four years later. As both were unmarried the line died out, but behind them the Walkers left a record of family mountaineering which has seldom, if ever, been equalled.

EDWARD WHYMPER

(1840 – 1911)

EDWARD WHYMPER WAS the first mountaineering name to be widely recognized by the general public, and such was the impact which he made that it is still the best known, a century later. How can this be, when the intervening years have seen such spectacular mountaineering successes as the ascent of Everest, and the grim battles with the north face of the Eiger? The answer is simple: Whymper was the first man to climb the Matterhorn.

Today, Whymper's route up the Matterhorn is not regarded as a very difficult climb and hundreds of people manage it each season, but its fame lingers on. The rumpus caused by the accident which occurred to Whymper's party on the descent, the mystery of the accident itself, and the publicity given to the climb by Whymper in his books and lectures have all combined to leave an indelible impression in the public mind.

Edward was the second of eleven children whose father was Josiah Wood Whymper, a respected artist and wood engraver of London. They were never a very prosperous family and the father and mother worked so hard to keep themselves respectable and financially solvent that young Edward was left very much alone during his formative years. He had a strange, withdrawn childhood, devoid of affection. He kept meticulous diaries (precision was a mania all his life—he kept an account of every halfpenny he spent) and these show him to be something of a prig, with no real friends. Undoubtedly this initial period of loneliness influenced his life—he was determined to make a name for himself.

He followed his father as an engraver and his first visit to the Alps, in 1860, was to make some sketches for the publisher William Longman, who was a member of the recently formed

Alpine Club and the man ultimately responsible for the famous *Alpine Journal*. Undertaking a long and comprehensive journey, Whymper visited in turn the Oberland, Valais, Mont Blanc and the Dauphiné. He did no real climbing, nor did he think much of the Matterhorn when he saw it.

Nevertheless he had a real feeling for the mountains and was able to express those feelings in his engravings. Longman was delighted—they were far and away the best mountaineering pictures produced at that time—so he asked Whymper to return to the Alps in the following year.

This time Whymper meant to climb. He began in Dauphiné with an ascent of Pelvoux, but in his mind he had already fixed on the idea of climbing one or other (or both) of the two highest unclimbed peaks still remaining—the Weisshorn and the Matterhorn. As he journeyed down the Aosta valley news reached him that Professor Tyndall had succeeded in climbing the Weisshorn and was about to attempt the Matterhorn. Alarmed at the thought of being thwarted of his ambition even before he had started, Whymper hurried up the Valtournanche towards the Matterhorn. He asked where he might find a guide and he was directed to the stonemason's house—a man known as Il Bersagliere, because he was once a soldier; Jean Antoine Carrel.

The meeting of Whymper and Carrel was one of the most fateful in Alpine history. Both instantly recognized in the other a man of equal mettle to himself. They met and clashed immediately, broke company and did not re-unite until the following year. It was the start of a love-hate relationship between two very strong characters.

It could never have happened if Carrel had been a guide in the proper sense, that is, a man who was dependent upon tourists for his living. But Carrel wasn't a guide—not in those days—just a peasant with above average intelligence, a passionate love of his native Italy and a strong desire to climb the Matterhorn. Above all, he wanted to climb the mountain from Italy and for Italy. He had no intention of allowing foreigners to come and take the prize from him, or even share it with him.

Then why did he help Whymper, as he did on numerous occasions? Perhaps it was because he recognized in the young engraver a fanaticism to equal his own, the one man who might rob him of the Matterhorn, and he thought it wise to keep close to him. Or it may have been that strange bond of respect which the two had for one another.

Suffice to say that for three years Whymper and Carrel tried in vain, either singly or together, to climb the Matterhorn. Strangely enough, the only other big mountain they tried together at this time was the Dent d'Hérens and they failed on that too. It was the only mountain which Whymper tried where he failed to reach the top.

In 1864 Whymper teamed up with Michel Croz, a dark little guide from La Tour near Chamonix; one of the finest of his day. Whymper always had a tremendous regard for Croz. 'Of all the guides with whom I ever travelled,' he confessed years afterwards, 'Croz was the one who was most after my own heart.'

They formed two members of a very strong party for an assault on the almost unknown region of Dauphiné, at the southern end of the Alps. The others were Moore and Horace Walker, and the great guide Christian Almer.

In a whirlwind tour they crossed various new passes and made the first ascent of the Ecrins. Walker then left them but the others continued to Chamonix where they were joined by the rich Irishman, Adams-Reilly, who was making a map of the area. Principally to help Adams-Reilly they made ascents of the Argentierè, Trélatête, and Mont Dolent; all new climbs.

Meanwhile Moore and Almer had gone ahead to Zinal where Whymper and Croz joined them. The way to Zermatt was blocked by the high ridge of the Weisshorn–Ober Gabelhorn chain through which they decided to force a pass. It was a memorable expedition and Whymper's engraving showing Croz flogging away at the huge cornice which greeted them, is one of the finest he made. Both Whymper and Moore agreed that had there not been two guides of the quality of Croz and Almer, the climb could never have been done. It is interesting to note though, that the third great guide of the period—Melchior

Anderegg—made sure that he crossed the pass the following year with his employers, the Walkers. It was not like Big Melchior to miss a new route!

By the start of the 1865 season Whymper was one of the acknowledged masters of Alpine climbing. Nothing he attempted seemed to defeat him and he entered on the new season with a swinging verve that made even his previous best seem child's play. Accompanied by three fine guides—Croz, Almer and Biener—he traversed the Grand Cornier, made a new and desperate attempt on the Dent Blanche (which ever after Whymper maintained was the hardest climb he had made) attempted the east face of the Matterhorn and was nearly swept away by an avalanche of rocks, climbed the Aiguille Verte and the Grandes Jorasses as far as the Pointe Whymper. Taken together with several high cols and the lovely but remote peak of La Ruinette, this constituted 100,000 feet of climbing in eighteen days, much of it new. It is a feat without parallel in alpine history.

But hard on the heels of this success came the first hint of the tragedy which was soon to follow. Owing to a mix up in their arrangements Croz was forced to leave Whymper for another employer. Though he still had Almer and Biener neither were anxious to try the Matterhorn again and so Whymper was once more thrown on to the services of Jean Antoine Carrel.

The story of those last few fateful days which led to the conquest of the Matterhorn and the ensuing accident has been told time and again. There are so many ifs and buts, so many coincidences and complications that it still forms a subject of speculation.

Briefly, the first complication arose because Carrel had already made arrangements to climb the mountain with a party of Italians, but without fixing a date. By pure coincidence the date coincided with that he had agreed with Whymper, and so, apologetically, he broke his agreement with the Englishman. Whymper did not know that Carrel intended to try the mountain —he thought his arrangements were to conduct a family on a glacier tour—but when he found out the truth, he flew into a terrible rage. He was stranded in the valley with no guides, forced to watch the Italians attempting the climb which he considered to be rightly his.

Again coincidence. Just when Whymper's cause seemed lost Lord Francis Douglas, a young man making a name for himself as a climber, arrived from Zermatt. Whymper persuaded him to return and help him climb the Matterhorn from the Swiss side—a route which had never been seriously tried before. Once there they employed the Taugwalders, father and son, to act as their guides for the expedition—though the Taugwalders were known to be mediocre men at their craft.

Again coincidence. Who should they find in Zermatt but Michel Croz! He had been freed from his engagement owing to the indisposition of his employer and now he had taken up with two men, the Rev. Charles Hudson and Douglas Hadow, for an attempt on the Matterhorn!

In the hotel that evening everyone agreed to join forces. Whymper was not too happy about the way things were turning out—the party was too big and young Hadow had virtually no experience—but there was nothing he could do about it.

On July 13 they climbed part way up the Hörnli ridge, amazed to discover how easy it was. They camped that night in jolly mood, and continued their journey next day. By 1.40 p.m. they were on the summit, and the long fight for the Matterhorn was over! Much to his satisfaction Whymper could see Carrel still a long way down the Italian Ridge. He and Croz hurled boulders down to let them know they were beaten.

Even so, as he watched Carrel retreat, Whymper felt pangs of regret. He felt that of all men, Jean Antoine should be the one to stand on the Matterhorn with him.

On the descent the accident happened which was to reverberate round the world. Hundreds of thousands of words have been written in the century since it happened seeking to explain it in rational terms. There are so many imponderables—why was Croz first man on the rope when as the best climber he should have been last during the descent? Why was an old rope used when there was plenty of new available? How much did the inexperienced Hadow contribute to the accident—did he really slip, and if so why were Croz and Hudson not holding him on a tight rope? We can never know the answers. The facts speak for themselves—four men came off on an awkward bit of the climb, the rope broke, and only Whymper and the Taugwalders remained alive to tell the tale.

It has been said that the Matterhorn accident held back the progress of mountaineering for many years, but this is not true. There was an awful outcry at the time, naturally, intensified by Whymper's initial refusal to make any statement concerning what happened, but it soon died down and there is no evidence to suggest that the accident stopped anyone from climbing. In fact, membership of the Alpine Club grew rapidly.

The ascent of the Matterhorn marked the end of the Golden Age of Alpine climbing. Of the really big peaks, only the Meije remained unscaled. Progress, when it came, was to assume a different form, and as if symbolic of this, on the very day after the Matterhorn was climbed, the Walkers and their companions made the first ascent of the Brenva Face on Mont Blanc, heralding a new era.

Whymper was only 25 at the time of the Matterhorn tragedy. He handled the scandal which ensued with the calmness of a man twice his age and he emerged from it with dignity and stature.

Ironically enough the Matterhorn tragedy enabled Whymper to live in comfort for the rest of his life. Engraving was a dying art, being ousted by photography, and his income came increasingly from his popular lectures and articles. He was a superb lecturer, never failing to draw large crowds wherever he went.

He also wrote *Scrambles Amongst the Alps*, a work which took him six years to complete, including his superb engravings. It was a revolutionary book for its day, because though it was not a literary masterpiece, it did breathe the very spirit of Alpine adventure and it still remains one of the truly great books on climbing.

Though he returned to the Alps almost every year after 1865

it was not to climb. His ascents were few, and the only one worthy of recall was his second ascent of the Matterhorn in 1874, which he made with his old antagonist Jean Antoine Carrel, his purpose being to obtain photographs for lecture slides. What a poignant moment it must have been as the two men stood together on the summit!

Whymper's interest turned to exploration and after two unfortunate expeditions to Greenland he went to the Andes, taking Carrel with him. They climbed Chimborazo and Cotopaxi, and though the former, at 20,498 feet, was the highest mountain climbed at that time, the main purpose of the expedition was scientific discovery.

Travels Amongst the Great Andes of the Equator which took him twelve years to write, never achieved the popularity of his earlier book, but it was a magnificent work which earned him high praise. Even *The Times*, one of his harshest critics in 1865, now described him as an explorer of the highest type.

In the meantime he had completed two guide books to Zermatt and Chamonix, intended for general tourists rather than mountaineers, and these achieved a steady popularity which helped his income over the years. He kept them meticulously up to date.

At the age of 61 he began a series of explorations in the Canadian Rockies for the Canadian Pacific Railway. Though he had a free hand to do more or less as he wished he ignored the many fine mountains which were waiting to be climbed. The old fire was gone.

In 1911 he went to the Alps on his usual summer round, paying calls at Geneva, Grindelwald and Zermatt before finally arriving at Chamonix early in September. On the 12th he did not feel well, locked himself in his room and refused medical aid. Four days later the old lion died, alone to the end.

FERDINAND IMSENG

(1845 – 1881)

IN THE YEARS following on the Matterhorn disaster there arose in the valley of Saas a group of guides who were destined to take part in some of the finest first ascents ever made. Their own rocky valley gave them a good grounding in that branch of the sport which was coming more to the fore and their ice-manship was equal to the standards previously set by the Ober-landers and Chamonix men. Their leader was the bearded Alexander Burgener, immortalized by Mummery in *My Climbs in the Alps and Caucasus*; another, and quite different personality was Ferdinand Imseng.

The Imsengs farmed one of the highest holdings in the Saas Tal, at Zermeiggern, where they seem to have made a pros-perous living. At any rate the children, Ferdinand and his younger brother Abraham, had the benefit of a formal educa-tion, which is more than most of their contemporaries could boast. Strangely enough, though they held the same name as Curé Imseng, who did so much for the valley in its early days, they were not related.

Ferdinand grew up to be a professional chamois hunter, like his friend Burgener, and it was because of his occupation that he left his native valley at the age of 20 to live in the adjacent Italian village of Macugnaga, since the hunting season allowed by law was longer on the Italian side of the frontier. During the close season he worked in the mines of the Val d'Anzasca in the shadow of Monte Rosa, the mountain above all others with which Imseng's name is linked.

Imseng responded to the call of the mountains from an early age. His *führerbuch*—the little booklet carried by guides in which employers could write comments—dates from 1863, when he would be 18 years old, and like most guides he began his mountain career as a porter, that is, the man who carried the heavy luggage for the rest of the party. The surprising thing in Imseng's case, however, is that he remained a porter for nine long years, his talents unrecognized by the climbing world in general.

Then in 1872 came his big chance. He persuaded Richard Pendlebury to attempt the unclimbed east face of Monte Rosa: an expedition which most of the leading climbers had rejected as being too dangerous. Even the great Oberland guide, Christian Almer, had turned it down, and Pendlebury was warned about attempting such a foolhardy climb with a man who was no more than a porter. But Pendlebury refused to be put off; he had faith in Imseng, perhaps because of the man's intense advocacy and fiery zeal.

The party which set out on July 22, 1872, comprised six men. Their leader was Imseng, proudly promoted to chief guide and he was supported by Gaby Spechtenhauser who was the Pendlebury brothers' constant guide-companion from the Ötztal in Tyrol. Then came their porter, Olerto, the two Pendlebury's and a friend, the Rev. C. Taylor.

They were faced with a climb of several thousand feet up a wall of snow and ice whose only rival in the Alps is the Brenva Face of Mont Blanc. Unlike the latter, however, Monte Rosa has no obvious lines of attack, no conspicuous ridges, only ribs of icy rock and complicated couloirs. By modern standards the technical difficulties are not extreme, but because of the uncertain snow conditions the route will always be one of danger.

For a successful ascent the snow must be hard and consolidated, the night cold, and modern climbers who attempt the route are often near the finish when the first rays of sun begin warming the face.

Haunted by the spectre of softening snow Imseng's party climbed steadily up, threading their way through seracs and over crevasses. At one point the snow actually started to slide around them, but it was not a real avalanche, only a superficial softening of the snow and they were able to continue on their way to the summit.

As an ice climb of first magnitude, Imseng's matched the Brenva route of seven years previous, but four years later he came back and with his brother as second guide, and Luigi Briosci as patron he climbed the face by a different route, even more difficult than the first. It took twenty-one hours of climbing, every moment taut with tension, not knowing what the fickle snow was going to do.

Six weeks after his first ascent of the east face of Monte Rosa Imseng arrived at Zermatt as the guide of George Passingham, an extremely fit young man who was one of the strongest goers the Alps has ever seen, and the climber to whom the now familiar term 'hard man' was first applied. With them was Franz Andermatten, a former neighbour of Imseng's and doyen of the Saas guides.

At the Monte Rosa Hotel they met Clinton Dent and Alexander Burgener and they were happy to fall in with Dent's suggestion that they should all attempt to climb the Zinal Rothorn from Zermatt—a pet scheme of Burgener's.

Nowadays, the Zinal Rothorn, which stands up as an impressive spire, is climbed more often from Zermatt than it is from Zinal, but in 1872 it was considered impossible by the Zermatt guides. This is probably why Burgener wished to try it in the first place, since there was no love lost between the men of Saas and Zermatt.

They made the ascent direct from the village with no trouble at all, but on the descent an accident occurred which nearly cost Imseng his life. They were descending an awkward slab and Imseng was going down first, unroped, as guides often did in those days. Suddenly, without warning, a large boulder peeled away from the top part of the slab and headed straight for him. By rights he should have been swept off the mountain but at the very last moment the boulder struck a projecting knob of rock and bounced clean over his head! Much shaken by this they lost no time in hurrying down, arriving back at the hotel in time for dinner.

The ascent of the Zinal Rothorn angered the Zermatt men so much that the bitter feelings between them and

the Saas guides, and especially Burgener, reached new proportions.

And of course, when Burgener and Mummery on the one
hand, and Imseng and Penhall on the other, made an almost
simultaneous ascent of the Zmutt Ridge of the Matterhorn, it
added even further to the Zermatter's wrath. This was another
climb which they had pronounced 'impossible'.

The Zmutt Ridge is such an obvious way of attempting the
Matterhorn that it positively cried out to be climbed, but such
was the fear engendered by the mountain, especially after
Whymper's accident, that nobody was willing to try anything
new on it. The attitude can be summed up by the great guide
Melchior Anderegg, who when asked whether the Zmutt would
go, replied 'Yes it goes—but I'm not going!'

Yet, by a strange twist of Fate, two parties were on the ridge
on the same day in 1879. How fortune wavered from one to the
other is told in more detail in Mummery's story. In short,
though, Mummery's party kept to the ridge all the way whilst
Imseng tried to beat them by a short cut on the west face.

Only a man of Imseng's temperament would have been bold
enough to suggest a route on the west face of the Matterhorn,
and only Penhall, a daring young medical student, would have
been rash enough to follow. It is acknowledged as one of the
most dangerous routes in the Alps, continually bombarded by
falling stones and involving the crossing of a notorious avalanche gully called Penhall's Couloir. As far as is known it has
only once been repeated.

It was all in vain—Mummery beat them to the top by an
hour and a quarter.

Though Imseng hated being beaten by anyone, he held no
animosity towards Burgener for the Zmutt affair, they were too
great friends for that. In fact, a few days later, Burgener,
Imseng, Penhall and Mummery climbed the easy Durrenhorn
together. The amusing thing is that these four men, the best
climbers of their day, were lost—they had mistaken the mountain for the Nadelhorn!

Despite his Swiss origins Imseng looked Italian, dapper and

moustachioed, and in his climbing he had undoubtedly acquired a Latin temperament. Mercurial, volatile, the fault against him was that when the chips were down he would throw caution to the winds. Imseng often rushed in where even angels feared to tread. Nevertheless, he had the stamp of greatness and his employers included the finest climbers of the day.

On August 8, 1881, Imseng set out with Signor Marinelli, a second guide and a porter to repeat the ascent of the east face of Monte Rosa which had first made him famous nine years before. Despite the warm day they climbed well up the great face looking for a bivouac site, ignoring the obvious avalanche dangers. Just before 5 p.m. the mountain seemed to fall apart, huge ice blocks and roaring tons of snow swept the whole face. When the debris settled only the badly shaken porter was left alive to stagger back to Macugnaga with the news that the great Ferdinand Imseng had perished.

WILLIAM CECIL SLINGSBY

(1849 – 1929)

IN THE SUMMER of 1872 a young Englishman stood on the Sognefjeld in Norway looking in amazement at the chaotic jumble of savage rock and ice which is the Horungtinder. Peaks seemed to fling themselves skywards at impossible angles from a maze of crevassed glaciers and high cols, each peak more aggressive than its neighbour. What a contrast it was to the ordered beauty of the Lakeland fells he knew so well! He was not in the least surprised when his guide informed him that the Horungtinder had never been crossed.

One mountain in particular caught his eye—the towering black obelisk of Skagastolstind. He was told it was the highest mountain in Norway (which was untrue) and that nobody had stood on its summit. There and then, he determined that he should be the one to climb it.

It could be argued that even if young William Cecil Slingsby had not chanced on that marvellous view of the Jotenheim moutains he would still have become a climber in the process of time, because he was brought up in an atmosphere of mountaineering, and this is probably true. As a boy he had tramped his native Craven hills with his cousins the Hopkinsons and Tribes, who were to play a major role in British climbing. Nevertheless, it was this chance trip to Norway which really fired his imagination.

Cecil Slingsby was born in 1849 into a family of Yorkshire squires whose pedigree stretched back for centuries. In the old days the family had something of a reputation for being swashbuckling, devil-may-care fellows who rode to hounds and quaffed their ale by the quart. They stood for God, King and Country and were quite ready to die for their beliefs—one of them did, in fact; Cromwell had his head cut off. When the nineteenth century brought riches to the new industrial middle class, the Slingsby's adroitly turned to textile manufacture, married into the influential Dewhurst family and settled down to become respectable Victorians. Nevertheless, the boundless energy was still there—and Cecil Slingsby inherited it in full measure.

He grew into a young man of magnificent physique and uncommon good looks, and, like his forebears, made a reputation as a huntsman of great skill.

Two years after his first visit to Norway he returned with his cousin, Algernon Dewhurst, and promptly made the first crossing of the fearful Horungtinder. This so amazed the locals that they looked upon Slingsby with awe as something between a god and a Viking, and indeed he was not unlike the latter with his massive frame and blond hair. He always claimed that there was in fact Norse blood in his ancestry.

He returned yet again in the following year when he made a number of first ascents of peaks with incredibly tongue twisting Norwegian names, but it was his campaign of 1876 which really earned him the title of Father of Norwegian Mountaineering.

For that season's climbing Slingsby teamed up with a Norwegian named Emanuel Mohn, who had already begun to explore his native mountains. Mohn was dazzled by Slingsby's crossing of the Horungtinder and Slingsby, for his part, realized that Mohn's local knowledge could prove invaluable. Together with a local reindeer hunter called Knut Lykken, who acted as guide, they made their way into the Horungtinder.

In a brilliant campaign they climbed six new summits in five days, until on July 21, they found themselves below the towering form of Skagastolstind.

The mountain was separated from the rest of the chain by a high col, now known as Mohn's Skar, from which descended the steep Slingsby Glacier. The col seemed to be the key to the ascent, and Slingsby, impatient to get to grips with it, unroped from his companions and hastened ahead.

When at last he struggled up the last steep ice slopes and stood on the col, his heart sank. From Mohn's Skar the peak rises in an apparently sheer block, 500 feet, and seemingly impregnable. As he stood looking at it his two comrades arrived and at once declared the ascent impossible.

Secretly, Slingsby was inclined to agree with them, but whether from sheer Yorkshire cussedness, or a bit of bravado, he declared out loud that he was going to try it. The other two declined to accompany him, but undismayed he set off alone and much to his surprise found that the climbing though certainly steep was not exceptionally difficult. He reached the summit triumphant.

During the course of his long life Cecil Slingsby visited Norway some sixteen times. No aspect of the landscape, the culture or the people's lives, escaped him—he was fascinated by it all. He learnt the language and the people took him to their hearts. They taught him how to ski—a mode of transport which in those days was peculiar to Norway and had not been fashioned into a sport, and he was almost certainly the first Englishman to master this exciting art. When in later years he was invited to unveil a memorial to Norwegian fishermen who had died in the First World War, his journey through the country was like a Royal procession. Truly it was said that Norway had two patron saints—St. Olaf and Cecil Slingsby.

Slingsby became a legend in Norway during his own lifetime, and even today, in the fastnesses of the Jotenheim, his memory is kept green. The Norwegians as a nation are intensely pro-British, and Cecil Slingsby certainly did more than most to bring about this happy state of affairs.

Related as he was to the Hopkinsons, it was inevitable that Slingsby should widen his mountaineering activities beyond the shores of his beloved Norway. He became a member of the Alpine Club and he also played a leading part in the newly emerging sports of rock-climbing and pot-holing at home.

His first Alpine season was in 1878 when he seems to have done little except make a guideless attempt on the north ridge of the Grand Cornier with Emile Javelle and the Rev. A. G. Girdlestone. In the following year he climbed the Weissmies without guides and followed this with a traverse of Castor and Pollux, a traverse of Mont Blanc which lasted twenty-two hours, a traverse of the Dent d'Hérens and an ascent of the Matterhorn.

From then on he divided his summers between the Alps and Norway and a list of his climbs would read like a guide-book to both places. His best work at this time was done in Arolla where he made the first ascent of the Central Summit of the Dents des Bouquetins and the first traverse of the Aiguilles Rouges. He also climbed a spectacular little needle called the Dent de Satarma, which is a well known tourist feature of the lovely Arolla valley.

In 1892 and 1893 Slingsby formed one of that brilliant band who foregathered at Chamonix under the inspired leadership of A. F. Mummery. He was then 42 years old, but fit as a lion and strong as ever. With Carr and Mummery he took part in the dramatic attempt to climb the north face of the Plan—an expedition which lasted fifty-four hours before ending in exhausting defeat. It was Slingsby's job to re-cut the steps on the descent, whilst Mummery guarded the rear, and with Carr virtually collapsed in the middle of the rope. They spent a bitter night on the ice slopes, no sleep and very little food, yet even towards the end of that exhausting ordeal Slingsby could still turn to Carr and remark happily, 'What a glorious climb this is!'

Slingsby was not only a good rock-climber but a superlative ice-man as well. He came to the rescue of his companions, Mummery, Hastings and Collie, when they had made the first ascent of the Requin together and found themselves on a dangerously steep and unknown glacier after nightfall. With a moon flitting through heavy cloud, giving just occasional glimpses of the route, Slingsby unravelled the intricacies of the ice as though he knew every step of the way. Mummery, who had poor eyesight and was virtually blind in the dark relied heavily upon Slingsby that night.

It was unfortunate that Slingsby returned to Norway in 1894 because he missed taking part in the first unguided ascent of the

Brenva Face by his three companions. His experience, too, might have stood them in good stead had he accompanied them on their ill-fated visit to the Himalaya in 1895 when Mummery lost his life.

If Slingsby had done no more than his Norwegian and Alpine climbs he would still have been assured of a niche in climbing history, but the fact is that this remarkable man played an equally leading part in the development of rock-climbing and pot-holing in Britain. Though this is not the place to tell the story of his underground adventures it is interesting to note that the club he helped to found, and of which he was for ten years the President—the Yorkshire Ramblers—is one of the very few devoted to both climbing *and* caving.

He began his climbing with the Hopkinsons and with a young friend he introduced to the sport, Geoffrey Hastings. Later he climbed with everyone of note and took part in an incredible number of first ascents. There can hardly be a climber in England who at some time or another, has never repeated one of Slingsby's routes.

Perhaps his most famous climb is the chimney named after him on Scafell in the Lake District. Slingsby, with Haskett Smith, Edward Hopkinson and Geoffrey Hastings climbed up the narrow gully called Steep Ghyll until they found a place where they could break out onto the face of the Pinnacle, one of the prominent features of the crag. Soon they came to a chimney, eighteen inches wide and almost vertical which was cut away below and difficult to get into. By standing on the shoulders of two companions Slingsby managed to effect a lodgement and wriggle his way up. Not until he had run out 110 feet of rope could he find a safe resting place, and call the others to follow.

It was an exceptionally daring lead for its time, with a very long run-out of rope. Nowadays, the climb is much easier, using modern aids and techniques.

In 1892 he seconded Solly on the first ascent of the Eagle's Nest Ridge, Great Gable, which was one of the hardest climbs of that time and which still retains a *severe* grade in modern guide-books. It is a very exposed route, with little protection, and was a *tour de force* when it was first climbed.

Slingsby not only made the first ascent of many of the popular climbs, but the second as well. In a period when transport is not the easy matter it is today, his achievements are quite remarkable.

Slingsby had a boyish enthusiasm capable of infecting others, making him the ideal person to spread the idea of climbing as a sport. He had the foresight to realize that climbing could not go on for ever being the preserve of a few rich men like himself, if it was to develop, and so he did all he could, by lectures and practical help, to begin new clubs. He was honorary member of practically every club in Britain and President of most at one time or another.

He climbed until he was well into his seventies and died peacefully in his home in 1929.

THE HOPKINSON BROTHERS

John Hopkinson   (1849 – 1898)
Alfred Hopkinson   (1851 – 1939)
Charles Hopkinson (1854 – 1920)
Edward Hopkinson   (1859 – 1921)
Albert Hopkinson   (1863 – 1949)

DURING THE SECOND half of the last century British mountaineering boasted several remarkable families whose exploits
have gone down in history. The Walkers and the Pilkingtons
figure elsewhere in this book—these and others helped materi-
ally to found the sport in Britain and the Alps. Perhaps the most
remarkable of all, and certainly the most tragic, were the five
Hopkinson brothers from Manchester.

Their father was a mill mechanic; a self-made man who by
hard work and flair prospered and became an Alderman and
eventually Mayor of his native city. Their mother was one of
the Yorkshire Dewhursts, related to the Slingsbys and Tribes,
and a love of the open moors was a long tradition on both sides.
The young Hopkinsons grew up with an intimate knowledge of
the Yorkshire dales and the Lakeland fells. Little wonder that
they soon became involved in the new sport of rock-climbing.

It was a remarkably talented family even in an age where
talent seems to have been round every corner. Quite apart from
their climbing, which to the Hopkinsons was never more than a
mere diversion, each of the brothers achieved distinction in his
own chosen profession. The intellectual calibre of the family
was of the highest class.

John, the eldest, was a consulting engineer with a brilliant
academic career—Senior Wrangler at Cambridge, Doctor of
Science, London; Fellow of the Royal Society; and twice President of the Institute of Electrical Engineers. He was one of
the founders of modern electrical engineering, perhaps best

AIGUILLE DU DRU · The west and north faces of the Petit Dru.
In the background, the Verte.

SKYE : THE BLACK CUILLIN ABOVE GLEN BRITTLE · This glen, the mecca of climbers in Skye, is dominated by Sgurr Alasdair (3251 ft), the highest peak of the Cuillin.

THE JOTENHEIMEN, NORWAY · The scene which first aroused Slingsby's interest in climbing.

known to the public as the man who built Liverpool's famous
tram system which was such a feature of that city until shortly
after the Second World War.

His brothers Charles and Edward were also engineers and
the three of them frequently worked together on projects.
Edward it was who first introduced London to underground
electric trains in 1890—the start of the present tube system.

The other two brothers broke with the family tradition of
engineering. Sir Charles Hopkinson was lawyer, M.P., and
Vice Chancellor of Manchester University. Albert, the youngest
brother, became a leading Manchester surgeon and was eventually persuaded to become a lecturer in Anatomy at Cambridge, because, as he put it, 'it looks as though Cambridge
found it could not do without a Hopkinson'—a reference to the
strong ties which the family had established with the university.

They were a very closely knit band and when Charles was
elected Treasurer of Lincoln's Inn, with the necessity to choose
a crest and a motto he consulted his brothers as to what the
motto should be. It is significant that they chose *Who Shall
Separate Us?*

But even amongst brothers such as these one is the accepted
leader and there is no question that John Hopkinson, eldest and
near genius, was looked up to by his brothers with something
akin to reverence. John was the pivot of all their adventures
and the centre of their own little world.

The Hopkinsons were amongst the earliest of British rock-
climbers, and though their beginnings in the field are obscure,
because they kept no records, it is certain that they descended
the east face of Tryfan in Wales in 1882—four years before
Haskett Smith climbed Napes Needle, which is the generally
accepted start of the sport. Their interests soon turned to the
Alps, however, where along with other climbs they made new
routes on the Unterbachhorn and the Fusshörner.

Their first significant contribution to British climbing came
in the September of 1887 when Charles, Edward and Albert,
with their cousin, W. N. Tribe, attempted to descend the steep
face of Scafell Pinnacle. They were stopped at a point about

3

250 feet above the screes, on a narrow ledge. At this point Edward Hopkinson erected a pile of stones.

Hopkinsons' Cairn became a magnet for the best climbers of the day. Attempt after attempt was made to reach the tantalizing pile of stones from below; they seemed to offer a mocking challenge, so near yet so far. Charles himself led the first attempt in the December of the same year but he failed after climbing about 150 feet because of ice on the rocks.

On September 23, 1903, an experienced party led by R. W. Broadrick, who had made the first ascent of the difficult Broadrick's Crack on Dow Crag the previous year, attempted to reach Hopkinson's Cairn. For some unaccountable reason Broadrick relinquished the lead part way up which was taken by a climber called Garrett. The four men were not using belaying tactics, then not fully understood, but were spreadeagled across the sheer rock face, quite unprotected. Suddenly Garrett slipped and fell. One by one the others were plucked from their holds.

Another party, led by W. E. Webb, was on the cliff at the same time but they neither saw nor heard anything of the accident until later in the day when they returned to the ledge near Deep Ghyll to pick up the knapsacks they had left there. To their horror they discovered four bodies lying spread across the screes. Only a young man called Ridsdale was alive, though even he was in terrible condition. Webb and a companion tried to comfort Ridsdale as best they could whilst a third man raced to the valley for help. Unfortunately Ridsdale succumbed to his injuries before they got him down to the inn.

The 1903 accident remains to this day one of the greatest single tragedies to occur on the British hills. Hopkinson's Cairn was not attained until 1912 when the incomparable Herford, climbing in stockinged feet, ran out 130 feet of rope on the crucial pitch.

The Hopkinsons themselves found a much easier way to the top. Scrambling up the easy Deep Ghyll, on the right of the Pinnacle, they gained access to a deep rift which they called Professor's Chimney, in honour of John.

In 1888 Edward Hopkinson was one of the party led by Slingsby which made the first ascent of Scafell Pinnacle by the route now known as Slingsby's Chimney. In the same year he also seconded Geoffrey Hastings on the first ascent of the Great Gully of Dow Crag, a huge but lonely crag near Coniston. Later in the same year he returned with his brothers to this climb and led the first pitch direct—a severe climb which Hastings had avoided.

There can be little doubt that much of the Hopkinsons' climbing went unrecorded and it is a fair criticism of them that they failed to appreciate the part they were playing in the formation of a new sport. In fact their greatest 'discovery' was not recorded for three years—the northern face of Ben Nevis, which they explored in 1892.

It was only after Norman Collie had visited Ben Nevis in 1894, and climbed Tower Ridge, that the Hopkinsons, in the *Alpine Journal*, confessed that they had been there two years previously. They had made the first ascent of North East Buttress and the first descent of Tower Ridge. They had tried to climb Tower Ridge—it is the most prominent of the great ridges which are such a feature of the mountain—but they were stopped by the Great Tower. These were the first recorded rock-climbs on the Scottish mainland.

In 1895 the brothers returned to Dow Crag where they made the two climbs by which they are best remembered. Edward and John, with a climber named Campbell, climbed a severe and strenuous crack called Intermediate Gully. On the same day Charles was leading Hopkinson's Crack, a hard climb which commands respect even by present day experts.

The Hopkinsons were beginning to show a mastery of skill and technique which would have made them serious rivals to the great Owen Glynne Jones who was then establishing himself as the finest climber in the Lake District. Unfortunately, the promise was never fulfilled—stark tragedy was looming for this brilliant family.

The summer of 1898 saw John Hopkinson, with his wife and family of four sons and two daughters staying at Arolla in

Switzerland. They did a number of the popular climbs including the difficult direct ascent of the Aiguille de la Za. On August
27, the father with his son Jack, aged 18, and his two daughters,
aged 23 and 19, set out to traverse the well known Petite Dent
de Veisivi. When they did not return that evening a search
party set out and the next morning their bodies were found
below the south face of the mountain. They had obviously
fallen from somewhere near the top—they may have been trying
a new route, but it was impossible to tell what had caused the
accident.

It was a shattering blow to such a devoted family. The
remaining four brothers rushed out from England to the scene
of the tragedy but their was nothing they could do to lessen
their grief. John, their favourite, was gone. They never climbed
again.

*   *   *

It might be argued that mountaineering had caused a sense-
less waste of brilliant lives in the death of John Hopkinson and
his family. But who knows what dangers lie ahead even for
non-climbers? It is a sad postscript to this story to relate that
both of John Hopkinson's remaining two sons were killed in the
First World War.

THOMAS CLINTON DENT

(1850 – 1912)

EARLY IN THE August of 1870 a young man strode purposefully up the winding dust-covered track which led from Stalden to Eisten in the Saas Tal. He was a slightly built fellow, though tall, with a face which radiated sharp intelligence and shrewdness, and large hands showing promise of great strength. His clothes were that of the mountaineer and he wore boots which he had designed himself, and which hurt him considerably. His name was Clinton Dent.

Despite his comparative youth he was no stranger to the Alps. In five seasons he had graduated from walking and scrambling amongst the lower hills, to doing longer and more ambitious climbs with guides. Now, at the age of 19, he reckoned he was ready to try new conquests.

The trouble was there was scarcely anything left to conquer— or so the experts were saying. Of the really big peaks only the Meije remained virgin. It was not a very exciting prospect for one just starting!

But every generation sees old mountains in a new light. The pioneers were so intent on peak bagging that the means of ascent were held to be of very little account. Furthermore, the peaks they bagged had to be substantial things—4,000 metres preferably. Minor pinnacles they disregarded, and they included in this classification such notable summits as the Drus and the Géant!

It was Dent's generation who changed all that. They discovered that these so-called 'minor' summits were often much more formidable propositions to climb than the bigger mountains. Furthermore, they began to realize that simply to reach the top was not sufficient reward in itself, that the route itself was more important than the summit to a real climber.

How the stick-in-the-mud older members of the Alpine Club must have fumed when they read Dent's analysis of the situation in the *Alpine Journal: The older members of the Club have left us, the youthful aspirants, but little to do in the Alps. The Meije, the Géant, the Dru are for us, as the Schreckhorn, Wetterhorn and Matterhorn were for them. We follow them meekly, either by walking up their mountains by new routes or by climbing some despised outstanding spur of the peaks they first trod under foot. They have left us but these rock aiguilles. They have picked out the plums and left us the stones.*

His oblique comparison with *walking* up the old mountains and *climbing* up the new ones, must have been particularly galling to the pioneers!

Thomas Clinton Dent was born in 1850, the son of wealthy parents. Educated at Eton and Trinity he had no need to earn a living and for some years he spent his time in casual idleness playing all sorts of sport, usually badly, with summers in the Alps.

When he walked up to Eisten in 1870 he was going to meet another young man who was just beginning to make a name for himself as a guide—the bear-like Alexander Burgener.

They struck an immediate friendship, aiding and abetting one another in a number of schemes such as trying to build a hut above the Fee valley (Saas Fee, which is now the most popular of the villages in the Saas valley, and the nearest to the mountains, did not exist at that time, except as a collection of cow sheds) and indulging in some crazy climbs. Years later Dent recalled some of these youthful escapades with horror—he wondered that they escaped without injury.

In their initial season together they made the first ascent of the Lenzspitze; a fine pinnacle which is joined to the more substantial Nadelhorn by a high ridge. How they climbed it is something of a mystery: Dent did not describe the expedition for fourteen years, and when he did he claims they ascended the north buttress. Unfortunately, the Lenzspitze has no north buttress! What he probably meant was the north ridge, which rises from the Nadeljoch, a high col between the Lenzspitze and Nadelhorn, but there again, the Nadeljoch was not climbed until 1887, so Dent and Burgener must somehow have traversed across from the Nadelhorn, though Dent does not mention the latter peak at all in his account.

It must have been a most unsatisfactory route, and the chief cause for surprise is that they did not try the much more obvious east ridge, which is the way the peak is now climbed from Saas. The reason is probably that Burgener had tried this way before, during his days as a chamois hunter, and found it too difficult for his then undeveloped skill. In later years he would have romped up it!

In the following year they climbed the Matterhorn, the first time for either of them, and made the first ascent and traverse of the Portjengrat; a fine rock ridge above the Saas valley which has been a popular climb ever since.

The highlight of the next season was their meeting with Passingham and Imseng, described in Imseng's story, when they made the first ascent of the Zinal Rothorn from Zermatt. Dent often climbed with George Passingham after that, not seeming to mind the way in which the superbly fit young gymnastic instructor used to 'bomb' up and down mountains in record time. Passingham once climbed the Dom direct from his hotel in Zermatt (not even the nearest village!) and returned in time for dinner. Whenever Dent had a long, hard day, he always said he'd been 'doing a Passingham'.

In 1873 Dent and Burgener began the long campaign which was to end in the conquest of the Dru, that dramatic tower of rock which is one of the showpieces of Chamonix. Until that year nobody had tried to climb the mountain because it looked so inaccessible, but a few weeks before Dent arrived on the scene a strong party of five guides and five amateurs made a vigorous attack. They failed even to reach the ridge which connects the mountain with the mighty Verte.

Dent, Passingham, Burgener and Andermatten made their first attempt on a different line from that chosen by their predecessors, but met with no greater success. Undeterred, they tried again, using the original route, but they still failed. The Dru was obviously not going to be conquered without a struggle.

For two more years Dent tried to climb the mountain, but the summit seemed guarded by the demon of inaccessibility.

Then, quite suddenly, Dent gave up climbing! The reason was that at last he had decided what to do with his life—he was determined to become a doctor, and with a thoroughness which was typical of him he devoted all his energies to that end. In 1876 he entered St. George's Hospital Medical School as a student. It was a happy choice; when he qualified he joined the staff and ultimately became senior surgeon there.

But the call of the mountains was too strong for Dent to remain away for long. In 1878 he was back in Chamonix to take up the challenge of the Dru once again. Unfortunately, the season was one of the worst on record, and when September came round without any apparent improvement in the weather Dent returned to England, though he took the precaution of leaving Burgener and a friend, J. W. Hartley, on guard just in case things bucked up. No sooner had he arrived home than a telegram came telling him that a miracle had happened—the barometer was rising and the weather looked promising. Dent hurried back to Chamonix.

On September 11, 1878, Dent set out on his final attempt to climb the Dru. With him went Burgener and Hartley, with Kaspar Maurer as second guide. Before very long they reached their previous highest point from which they had to make an awkward stomach traverse to a niche below an ice-filled groove. The groove looked severe.

The two guides began exploring the groove, delicate bridging and backing-up on thin water ice, each man climbing by himself as was the custom of guides in those days—the ropes coiled round their shoulders for dropping to their employers after each pitch. Suddenly there was a sharp crack as a great flake of ice peeled off below Maurer's feet. His fingers slipped and he began to slide helplessly down the groove, when Burgener, with one massive paw, pinned him to the rock! It was an incredible feat on the part of the great Saas guide—standing bridged across an ice-filled groove, over an immense abyss, holding Maurer single-handed.

Soon, however, their difficulties were over, and at 12.30 p.m. they stood on the summit of the Dru. It had been Dent's nineteenth attempt.

Though Clinton Dent continued to visit the Alps and even climbed in Skye, it was the Caucasus which really attracted him in future years. He made four journeys there in all, including one to search for Donkin and Fox who had disappeared in 1888.

He also became increasingly concerned at the ever-growing number of climbing accidents, and he proposed that lives could be saved if a universal distress signal was invented like that used by ships at sea. He headed a committee to look into the subject and the answer they arrived at now forms the well-known Mountain Distress Signal, used throughout the world.

Dent was a very good photographer and a prolific writer of articles about mountaineering. He wrote two books—*Mountaineering* and *Above the Snow Line*—the first of which was the standard text-book on the subject for many years, though the second, an autobiography, never attained the popularity that Whymper's or Mummery's did.

It was only natural that a man of Clinton Dent's ability should be the recipient of many honours and hold high office in both the mountaineering and medical worlds. He never let these interfere with his innate commonsense and his great humanity. Though he spoke with an affected drawl, and was a noted wit, he was at heart a kindly man. He helped to shape modern climbing because he could see clearly the direction it was headed, and he was one of the first to recognize Mummery's genius and tried to get him elected to the Alpine Club.

At the beginning of August 1912 Clinton Dent caught a chill through playing cricket in the rain. Complications developed, and on the evening of August 26, after several days of semi-consciousness, he passed away quietly. Memorials to him were erected at the English Church in Zermatt and in the Britannia Hut which stands above Saas Fee, but his real memorial will always be the huge obelisk of granite which towers so splendidly above the Mer de Glace.

THE PILKINGTON BROTHERS

Charles Pilkington   (1850 – 1918)
Lawrence Pilkington (1855 – 1941)

ONE SUMMER'S DAY in 1869 two young boys, on holiday
in the Lake District, decided to scale Pillar Rock. They knew
nothing of rock-climbing, because the sport, as such, hadn't
been invented, but the elder of the two, Charles Pilkington, had
done some scrambling and reckoned he was equal to the task of
guiding his younger brother Lawrence up the formidable crag.
Before they reached the top—by the so-called 'easy way'—they
had more excitement than they ever dreamed of. It was the
start of one of the most notable climbing partnerships of the
nineteenth century.

Their youthful adventures on Pillar gave the Pilkingtons
something more than a love of climbing. The freedom with
which they climbed seemed equally important; it etched itself
into their unconscious and it may well have been the main-
spring which made them dispense with guides. Though they
were not the first guideless climbers, by any means, they were
amongst the best, and they did more than anyone else in their
day to break down the prejudice which existed at that time
against making ascents without guides.

The brothers came of well-known Lancashire stock. The
Pilkingtons could trace their name in Prestwich back to 1311,
and they owned several collieries in the Prestwich and Haydock
areas. They also owned a tile factory which was later to
grow out of all recognition into the immense Pilkington Glass
Co.

Charles was born in 1850 and Lawrence was five years his
junior, so that they were contemporaries of the other northern
families from the business world who were taking up mountaineering—people like the Walkers, the Hopkinsons, Slingsby

and Ellis Carr. Like these, the Pilkingtons found their exercise on the northern moors and in the mountains of the Lakes and Snowdonia, though at first it was walking, not climbing, which attracted them.

Both of the brothers were prodigious walkers and young Lawrence was the founder of the famous Fell Record in which a competitor has to cover the greatest distance possible and make as much ascent and descent as possible, within twenty-four hours. At the age of 16, accompanied by a Mr. Bennet, he undertook a Lakeland walk which included 12,900 feet of ascent in twenty-one hours, ten minutes. This record stood for twelve years until he joined his brother in another attempt, which pushed it up to 13,800 feet—though they were twenty-five minutes over the allotted time.

In the 1870's the brothers returned to the Pillar Rock hoping to climb it by one of its longer, sheer faces, but they were disappointed. Nevertheless, it was a notable try, a quarter of a century before its time.

In 1872 the Pilkingtons went to the Alps for the first time, employing two well-known guides. Unfortunately, they had only crossed a few passes when their holiday was brought to an end by Charles injuring himself whilst bathing in the Schwartzee, a little lake above Zermatt. Two years later they returned, and with the same guides climbed a number of the well-known routes.

In 1878 they began their two-season campaign in the Dauphiné, with their cousin Frederick Gardiner, which was to establish them as outstanding mountaineers. Dispensing with guides they made five first ascents and three second ascents and in addition the third ascent of the Rateau by a new route. Crowning it all they made the thirteenth and first guideless ascent of the Ecrins.

This was tremendous stuff, but a year later they excelled themselves by making the first guideless ascent of the Meije. It was the fourth ascent ever made of this peak, then regarded as the most difficult mountain in the Alps.

Two years later they added the Oberland and the Valais to

their areas of conquest: first guideless ascent of the Finsteraar-
horn and numerous other peaks including the Matterhorn.
Their finest achievement was the Jungfrau by the Guggi route,
which even today is regarded as a fairly difficult snow and ice
climb.

For the following year Gardiner's place was taken by Eustace
Hulton. This time they visited the eastern end of the Alps where
they made further first ascents on Piz Kesch, Piz Roseg and
Monte della Disgrazia.

As they continued their successful seasons in the Alps the
number of their climbs grew into a veritable catalogue, which
it would be impossible to repeat at length. The important thing
was that they made an astounding impact on other climbers—
for the first time they had proved conclusively that guides were
not necessary for experienced climbers, even on the most
arduous climbs. Unlike Girdlestone, who had had the temerity
to publish a book on guideless climbing some years before, the
Pilkingtons made no foolish mistakes. They influenced a whole
generation of climbers—men like Carr, Solly and Collie, and
eventually the great Mummery himself.

In 1880 the brothers went on a fishing trip to Skye, but finding the sport poor that year they turned their attentions instead
to the jagged range of the Black Cuillins. They were surprised
and delighted to find the climbing quite difficult.

At that time it was harder to reach the Cuillins than it was to
reach the Alps (in some respects it still is!). The mountains were
virtually unknown and unmapped, but Charles made a sketch
map and wrote enthusiastically about the climbing in the
Alpine Journal, so that others like Dent, Stocker and Parker, and
eventually the great Norman Collie were persuaded to try the
Cuillins themselves.

The Pilkingtons climbed the so-called Inaccessible Pinnacle
and the magnificent Pinnacle Ridge of Sgurr nan Gillean on
their first visit. A few years later they returned to make the first
ascent of Sgurr MhicChoinnich, Clach Glas and Sgurr na
h-Uamha. In honour of the work they did in discovering this
remote corner of Scotland one of the most shapely of the moun-

tains was named Sgurr Thearlaich, which is Gaelic for Charles's Peak.

Apart from Skye their contributions to the newly emerging sport of rock-climbing were small. With Hulton they made the first ascent of Deep Ghyll on Scafell in 1882, and Charles, with Horace Walker, made the first ascent of the west face of the remote Scottish mountain called Suilven. Though they were in a superb position to take part in the birth of homeland climbing Lawrence had the misfortune to injure himself when they were exploring the notorious gully of Piers Ghyll in 1884. He was badly crushed by a fall of stones. It left him virtually a cripple, and though he did manage some easy Dolomite climbs a few years later, it was really the end of his serious climbing.

Charles continued to climb regularly until 1911. His interest lay principally in Alpine rock climbs and he several times visited the Eastern Alps where rock climbs predominate. In the bigger ranges he would seek out the smaller rock pinnacles, such as the Aiguilles Rouges at Arolla or the Fusshörner. Usually his partners were men dedicated to guideless climbing like himself; Carr, Solly, and so on, but he also climbed a good deal with his great friend and neighbour, Horace Walker, who always brought along old Melchior Anderegg, the veteran guide who was practically a member of the family.

Before his death in 1918 Charles became President of the Alpine Club. He held many responsible positions in connection with the mining industry too, and it was probably the extra burden brought on by the First World War that led to his death.

His brother Lawrence lived on to become the Grand Old Man of British mountaineering. He died in 1941.

ALBERT FREDERICK MUMMERY

(1855 – 1895)

'HE WAS THE greatest climber of his or any preceding generation.'

In these words Martin Conway, himself no mean climber, unequivocably sums up the man who, more than any other single individual, set Alpine climbing on its present-day course.

A. F. Mummery was born on September 10, 1855, the son of a tannery owner who in due course became Mayor of his native Dover. He was not a prepossessing child: pale, thin and with a slight spinal deformity which gave him a weak back. Furthermore, he was very short sighted. Small wonder that all his life he hated being photographed.

Nevertheless, he was high spirited, extremely intelligent and witty and he seems to have been popular with other children. He was a born leader: he seemed to radiate that magic quality which made other men follow him without question. On the other hand he also made enemies easily, and his climbing career was marred by a clique that persistently tried to deny him recognition.

As a boy of 16 he paid his first visit to Switzerland and was entranced by the sight of the Matterhorn under a full September moon. The mystery and splendour of it caught his imagination and was the prime cause of everything which followed.

The Matterhorn was always his favourite mountain. He climbed it eight times by various routes. It was the scene of his first big triumph—the Zmutt arête—and, ironically, it was also his last Alpine climb before he went to the Himalaya.

Unlike Whymper, Mummery did not strike the Alps like a fireball. Whymper's career was concentrated into five short years—it was eight years before Mummery was even noticed. He built patiently, learning what he could from guides both good and bad, and above all testing his strength to see whether he could match the mountains. Apart from load-carrying, which his back made purgatory, he found he could manage as well as most guides. At rock climbing he was specially good, but long walks proved annoying because of his habit of climbing without spectacles which made it impossible for him to see the stones on the paths. He hated walking, and this was one of the factors which led to his death.

In 1879 he crossed the Tiefmattenjoch, saw the Zmutt arête of the Matterhorn and determined to climb it. All he required was a good guide, and fortune smiled on him—he was introduced to Alexander Burgener.

The previous year Burgener had made the first ascent of the Dru with Dent, confirming the fact that he was one of the best of the new breed of guides. What he thought of Mummery is not on record, but he certainly had no intention of trying the Zmutt arête with him. Instead, he insisted on a trial period, climbing the mountains near Saas. Mummery agreed.

With the young Augustin Gentinetta as porter they carried out a swift campaign against the Portjengrat, the Sonnigrat (first traverse) and the Fletschhorn, making a desperate route on this last mountain that nobody had the nerve to repeat for fifty-three years! It convinced Burgener that Mummery was a much better climber than appearances would suggest. He agreed to try the Zmutt.

They were almost robbed of their prize. By pure coincidence William Penhall, a daring young medical student, also had designs on the ridge and whilst Mummery and his guide rested in Zermatt Penhall set off for the Matterhorn with the brilliant, mercurial, Ferdinand Imseng as his guide.

The Zmutt arête consists of three parts: the lowest is a long and rather beautiful spine of snow set at an easy angle, then there are three sharp pinnacles known as the Zmutt Teeth and finally the ridge rears up very steeply towards the Italian summit of the Matterhorn. Penhall was stopped by the gap between the Teeth and the steep continuation of the ridge. After a night in the open, he decided to retreat.

On the way down to Zermatt Penhall met Mummery coming in the opposite direction. They passed the time of day and Penhall gave Mummery his opinion that the weather would break. Burgener and Imseng agreed that this was likely and urged Mummery to return to Zermatt, but he refused. Already his mind had seen a half chance of climbing the Zmutt, for if the weather remained good he wanted to be ready and waiting near the mountain.

Once again luck was with him. The weather stayed fine and though Penhall made a desperate dash back from Zermatt he had lost his chance. Mummery was on the ridge. It was then that Imseng made his fantastic route up the west face which is described elsewhere in this book.

Despite his tactical advantage Mummery almost didn't make the climb, and ironically enough it was Imseng who spurred him on to complete it. Mummery's party were stopped by the same awful gap which had stopped Penhall, and Burgener thought the way ahead looked too dangerous. He counselled retreat, but at that moment a yodel told them that Penhall and Imseng had returned to do battle, and this was too much for Burgener's fighting spirit. He had no intention of being beaten by Imseng.

What a fantastic day that was on the Matterhorn! On the one hand Penhall's party clambering up the west face and being bombarded by stones, on the other hand Johann Petrus soloing up the ridge, followed by Burgener and Mummery roped together with Gentinetta bringing up the rear, and like Petrus, unroped. Nowadays such behaviour would be called criminal folly, but at that time the use of the rope for protection was only vaguely comprehended even by the best climbers.

The race for the Zmutt led to a friendship between Mummery and Penhall, and it was probably the latter who suggested Mummery should join the Alpine Club. Unfortunately, a clique existed who were jealous of Mummery's success: they sent out rumours about him which were quite untrue but which were sufficient to get him blackballed—in those days one black ball in ten was sufficient for exclusion.

Some might have shrugged off such an insult—for insult it was—but Mummery was a man with a sensitive nature and it hurt him deeply to be rejected by his fellow climbers. Indeed, his continuing exclusion from the Club almost led to him giving up climbing altogether. Eight long years were to pass before he gained admittance.

The year following upon the Zmutt success was a vintage one for Mummery. With Burgener he made the first crossing of the Col du Lion, a fearsome ice couloir on the Italian ridge of the Matterhorn, and then, adding little Benedikt Venetz to his party, made the first ascent of the rocky pinnacles of the Charmoz above Chamonix. They also had two notable failures —the Furggen Ridge of the Matterhorn and the monolithic Géant, in the Mont Blanc range.

1881 saw the conquest of the Grépon; the expedition for which Mummery is perhaps best known. He had climbed the Charpoua face of the Verte by a dangerous route with Burgener whilst Venetz was ill, but once all his forces were gathered together again he concentrated on the Grépon.

The spires of Grépon, so easily seen from Chamonix, had defeated all attempts to climb them. In the previous year, Mummery when he scaled the adjacent Charmoz had taken a good look at the Nantillons side of the Grépon and decided that it could not be climbed that way. In 1881, therefore, he first went round to the other side of the mountain, overlooking the Mer de Glace, and tried from there. He was not successful. The climbing was much more difficult than he had expected, and Mummery was not prepared to bivouac for the night— had he done so he might well have climbed it, for it was within the party's capability. As it was, the Mer de Glace face of Grépon had to wait for Young, thirty years later.

Defeated by the Mer de Glace face, Mummery returned to the Nantillons side and discovered to his surprise that it was not so difficult after all. The key was a big crack, now called the Mummery Crack, which gave access to the long jagged ridge of the mountain.

On that first attempt they went as far as the north summit,

but Mummery suspected, quite rightly, that a pinnacle a little further to the south might be even higher and thus the true summit. Two days later, therefore, he returned and climbed the whole route again, this time pushing further on until he came to the south summit. The ascent of this spire was done by means of a formidable crack, led by Venetz.

Shortly after this Mummery became involved in a row with the Rev. W. A. B. Coolidge who was the editor of the *Alpine Journal*. To most men this would scarcely have mattered since Coolidge was notorious for falling out with people, but it seems to have come near to breaking Mummery's spirit. For five years he gave up serious mountaineering.

In the meantime he married, and when he returned to his old haunts it was with his wife as companion. In 1887, with Burgener and Andermatten, he and his wife made the first ascent of the Täschhorn by the Teufelsgrat. As it turned out it was a very serious undertaking—the ridge is long and very rotten, and both guides were injured during the climb. They were on the mountain for twenty-eight hours.

The following season he went to the Caucasus with the guide Heinrich Zurfluh of Meiringen and climbed Dych Tau (17,054 feet) the second highest mountain in the region and the highest unclimbed peak in Europe at that time. That same year he was at last elected to the Alpine Club.

Once again he dropped out of the limelight for a few seasons, making only minor ascents. The fact is, he was undergoing a great period of rethinking, not only about his climbs but about his life in general. Already he had become deeply involved in questions of political economy which took a good deal of his time and he was considering whether to retire from business in order to devote all his energies to economics. He was also beginning to realize the limitations of guided climbing.

In 1891 he met Ellis Carr and Martin Conway. Conway offered him a place on his forthcoming Karakorum Expedition but Mummery's ideas of climbing were not those of Conway— the latter was leading a vast and expensive expedition whose job was more scientific and geographical than anything else, and

Mummery, though he longed to visit the Himalaya, had little interest in such matters. His sole interest in mountains was the climbing of them.

The meeting with Carr confirmed his ideas about guideless climbing. Together they made some new routes in the Graians and arranged to meet at Chamonix the following season.

In 1892 Mummery began the second great phase of his career when he became the leading advocate of climbing without guides. For one whose considerable reputation rested on his partnership with Burgener, it was a bold step.

At Chamonix that year there was a brilliant company of amateurs; men with a long string of successes both in the Alps and on the crags of Britain. Yet these men willingly elected Mummery their leader, for already he was something of a legend.

Their first climb was a bold attempt on the north face of the Aiguille du Plan; a very steep hanging glacier directly facing Chamonix. Today it is climbed by way of a rocky spur in its lower section, but Mummery could not find the key to this obvious though difficult line of attack and so, with Slingsby and Carr, he embarked on a steep couloir which flanks the rock buttress to its left.

The climbing was of the severest kind; very steep ice in a dangerous couloir, but Mummery led it without hesitation. Once above the couloir they expected the going to be easier but in this they were disappointed and when night fell they were still a long way from the top. Dressed only in normal summer clothing ('my jacket was unlined,' Carr noted later), they spent a miserable night crouched on the ice wall. In the morning Carr was too exhausted to continue and there was nothing for it but to descend.

The thought of the couloir filled them all with dread, but once again Mummery rose to the occasion. At the top, where it was steepest, he descended on a rope, cutting steps for his companions until he reached a place of comparative safety. Then he climbed up again and lowered them down on the rope after which, completely unprotected, he calmly came down as last man.

In the opinion of Slingsby, it was the finest piece of climbing he had ever witnessed. Certainly the attempt on the Plan north face was one of the most daring ice climbs attempted at that time. The face was not climbed until 1924.

It took ten days for them to recover from their attempt on the Plan, but then came the first traverse of the Charmoz by a party which included two ladies, Miss Bristow and Miss Pasteur. On August 18 came the classic traverse of the Grépon, with Hastings, Collie, and Pasteur.

It was the first time anyone had looked at the north ridge of the Grépon since the ascent by Mummery eleven years earlier. The question now was, could Mummery climb his eponymous crack? In fact, he led it without difficulty. Fortunately, though, the final difficult crack to the summit was avoided because Pasteur knew of an easier route.

Later in the season Mummery once more teamed up with a guide—the famous Emile Rey of Courmayeur—in an attempt on the Hirondelle Ridge of the Grandes Jorasses. They failed at the *mauvais pas*, an awkward step in the ridge, principally because the rocks were icy. The ridge was not climbed until 1927.

After making the second ascent of the notorious Great Gully of Wastwater Screes, which put him off Lakeland climbing for ever, Mummery returned to the Alps in 1893 and with Slingsby, Collie and Hastings climbed a sharp unnamed peak which Collie christened the Dent du Requin—the Shark's Tooth. They also climbed the west face of the Plan, as some recompense for their failure on the north face the previous year.

In 1894 Slingsby returned to his beloved Norway but Hastings and Collie were with Mummery again, blazing an astonishing trail. Nothing seemed too difficult for them: the Col des Courtes, a severe ice climb seldom repeated, the Verte by the Moine Ridge, which they thought was a new route but which had been done in 1865, and the first guideless ascent of the Brenva Face of Mont Blanc.

The Brenva climb was a magnificent achievement. In the

thirty years since its first ascent it had only been climbed on four other occasions and always by first-rate guides. From 1894 nobody could doubt that the *best* amateurs and the *best* guides could count themselves equal.

As a finish to the season Mummery returned to Zermatt and repeated his ascent of the Zmutt arête. It was his last Alpine climb.

For some years he had longed to visit the Himalaya but it was not until 1895 that he found it possible to fulfil this wish. In that year, with Collie and Hastings, he set off intending to climb Nanga Parbat (26,620 feet).

It is easy for us, with our superior knowledge of high altitude climbing based on the experience of many expeditions, to laugh at the idea of three Victorian climbers trying to climb a mountain like Nanga Parbat, but we must remember that Mummery and his companions did not have our knowledge. They really were pioneers in every sense of the word and there is little doubt that they regarded the Himalaya simply as bigger and better Alps. They chose Nanga Parbat, which has since proved to be the toughest of all the big Himalayan peaks and unclimbed until 1953, simply because it was easily accessible.

They learnt slowly, the hard way. They were benighted, lost and exhausted on more than one occasion. They suffered the rigours of climate, altitude and poor food. But they put up a magnificent effort.

Bruce, the young officer who trained Gurkhas, had joined them and it was with one of Bruce's men, Raghobir, that Mummery reached over 20,000 feet on the Diamiri Ribs—stupendous climbing which according to Collie was as difficult as the west face of the Plan. It can certainly be included amongst the most difficult rock climbs ever tried at high altitudes, and ever since Mummery's time it has been a tempting bait for expeditions—though most of them wisely resisted the temptation! It was climbed by a German party in 1962.

With their holiday almost at an end a decision was made to move camp to another valley so that they could see the only face of the mountain they had so far not explored. The move meant a long walk round a spur and this was not to Mummery's liking. He proposed to cross the spur direct.

Collie didn't like the idea at all and he cautioned Mummery to take great care. The spur was steep and icy and there was no means of knowing whether descent was possible on the other side.

Mummery laughed at his fears. 'Don't worry—I'm not going to risk anything for the sake of an ordinary pass,' he said.

On the morning of August 24, 1895, Mummery and two Gurkhas set off to make the crossing. They were never seen again.

We shall never know how Mummery died, though the chances are that he was swept away by an avalanche. It can be argued that the scale of the Himalaya defeated him, that he failed to learn anything even in the few weeks he was there and that this is what really killed him.

He left behind his reminiscences *My Climbs In The Alps and Caucasus*, which, along with Whymper's *Scrambles* is one of the best known of the early climbing books. In it he gives his philosophy of climbing, that adventure and danger are complementary and that there cannot be one without the other. The essence of mountaineering is not to avoid danger but to acquire sufficient skill to overcome it.

He also left behind the memory of a dynamic personality whose impact and influence went far beyond his actual achievements, great though those were. Nobody, before or since, has had such a profound impact on the sport of climbing.

LILY BRISTOW

LILY BRISTOW WAS a most spirited young lady. In an age when females took chaperones to church she camped out quite blatantly with members of the opposite sex, even sharing tents! It was enough to cause a scandal in her middle-class Exeter home, though apparently it never did. Lily no doubt grew up to be a good wife and mother in some Victorian town house, taking tea with the vicar and attending mothers' meetings, but for a few brief years she flashed across the world of mountaineering like some bright little comet.

The Bristows were friends of the Pethericks and Lily was the confidante of Mary Petherick, who, in 1883, married Fred Mummery. There can be little doubt that Mummery jolted the cosy Exeter atmosphere out of any complacency it might have had—he was that sort of person—and one effect was to make Mary, her brother, and Lily Bristow, into keen climbers.

Exactly when Lily started climbing is not certain, and of course, at this period Mummery's activities are unknown, but it would be fair to assume that at least part of the time was spent in the Alps with his wife and their friends. She first comes into prominence in 1892 when she turned up with the family at Chamonix and took part in the mass assault on the Charmoz. What a day that must have been! The Charmoz ridge must have looked like the scene of some extraordinary garden party —five men and two ladies scrambling along the narrow crest. It is all the more surprising when one considers that the Charmoz at that time was still considered a difficult mountain even for the most experienced mountaineers. For Miss Bristow and Miss Pasteur, the other lady, it was a considerable achievement.

Miss Bristow, however, was only getting into her stride. The

following season she was back at Chamonix with the Mummerys, where they were joined by Fred's three favourite companions—Slingsby, Collie, and Hastings. The four men were
probably the best combination then climbing in the Alps and it
says much for Lily Bristow that she was allowed to accompany
them on all but two of their climbs. She was not taken on the
first ascent of the Requin nor the west face of the Plan, much to
her chagrin, no doubt.

Her most celebrated achievement, however, was the traverse
of the Grépon. The climb had been done once only, by Mummery the previous year, and it was considered the ultimate in
rock-climbing. Not only did she manage it under less than ideal
conditions but she took along with her a heavy plate camera and
photographed the expedition. It was this climb by Lily Bristow
that caused Mummery to make his famous comment about how
the hardest climb in the Alps soon becomes an easy day for a
lady.

Lily was thrilled with the climb. 'It was more difficult than I
could ever imagine,' she wrote home. 'A succession of problems,
each one of which was a ripping good climb in itself.' They
came down from the peak very late, got lost on the Nantillons
glacier in the pouring rain (Lily borrowed Mummery's cloak and
was the only dry member of the party) and six climbers were
forced to spend the night cramped in a tent designed for two.
So crowded was it that only Lily was allowed the luxury of
lying down—the men sat huddled together, waiting for dawn.

Not content with having traversed the Grépon, she next set
her sights on the Petit Dru. On this expedition she was even
allowed to lead for a time—'It's so much more fun,' she said.
The Dru at that time was regarded as a test piece for experts,
second only to the Grépon.

From Chamonix the Mummerys moved to Zinal and Lily
went with them, whilst Slingsby and the others took the so-
called High Level Route across the mountains to Zermatt. At
Zinal she persuaded Mummery to climb the Zinal Rothorn,
much against his wishes, because the Rothorn is a long way from
the village and Mummery hated walking. During the long slog

up the valley he repeatedly suggested they should turn back but he was no match for Lily's feminine wiles; she was determined to climb the Rothorn even if she had to argue with him all the way to the top!

When they got back to Zinal after a successful ascent, the Swiss guests at the hotel refused to believe that Miss Bristow had been to the top of the Rothorn. They smiled politely, telling her that it was quite impossible—obviously she had mistaken some small hillock for the great mountain.

Any suggestion that Lily was a fair-weather climber was dispelled when later in the season she made an ascent of the Italian Ridge of the Matterhorn with 'the boys' as she called her distinguished companions. On the way down they were caught in a violent storm and what had begun as a light-hearted expedition turned into a savage fight for survival. They reached the valley utterly exhausted, but Lily's enthusiasm was in no way dimmed by the experience.

From her letters home it is quite clear that Lily Bristow had a 'crush' on Mummery, which is hardly surprising. Mummery and his companions were heady company for anybody, let alone an impressionable young girl. It may be that Mary Mummery tried to discourage her—at any rate Lily did not climb with Mummery the following year.

Instead, she made the first descent of the Zmutt ridge with the guides Zurbriggen and Pollinger—only the fourth time the ridge had been climbed, though by a curious coincidence it was climbed twice again on the same day that Lily descended it. It was a very great accomplishment for a lady climber and placed Lily Bristow among the leading climbers of the day.

Unfortunately, at this point her climbing ended. Would she have gone on to become a great leader of guideless climbs—the first woman to lead the Drus or the Grépon, perhaps? She certainly had that potential.

But we shall never know. In the following year Mummery vanished on Nanga Parbat, and Lily Bristow's little world was shattered.

WILLIAM MARTIN CONWAY

(1856 – 1937)

WHEN THE SMALL boy standing on the summit of Snowdon found that he could not reach the top of the cairn to place another stone there, he was not in the least dismayed. At a signal from him, a butler stepped forward and performed the task.

This fortunate youth was William Martin Conway; a child born with a silver spoon and destined by the Gods to be favoured in all he did and was.

Born on April 12, 1856, of wealthy parents, Conway grew up with the stature and looks of an Adonis, an outstanding intelligence and a flair for adventure. He swept majestically through the late Victorian climbing scene like some latter-day Walter Raleigh, except that Conway was much more successful than his Elizabethan counterpart. Everything he touched turned to gold; failure was something that happened to others.

After coming down from Cambridge, Conway toured the principal libraries of Europe in an extensive study of early printing and engraving. He wrote books of art criticism and became successively Professor of Art at the University College of Liverpool and later Slade Professor of Fine Art at Cambridge. Art and mountaineering dominated his life.

Conway began climbing at a time when men were turning their attentions to new ways up old mountains. It was often a frustrating business because not infrequently a party would return to the valley only to discover that their difficult 'new route' had in fact been done before but not recorded. Conway himself was a victim of such a mistake on Monte Rosa in 1877 and this so annoyed him that he determined to compile a list of all the known climbs round Zermatt, so that others should not be similarly inconvenienced.

So began the first real climbers' guide-book. It is ironical to note that the original intention was to indicate the routes which had been accomplished in order to *avoid* them, but of course, it soon found its use as a guide-book in the proper sense.

Conway was helped in his task by the Rev. W. A. B. Coolidge, then the Editor of the *Alpine Journal*, and a walking encyclopedia of Alpine knowledge. The slim volume was entitled the *Zermatt Pocket Book* and appeared in 1881.

Despite its moderate price of half-a-crown, and its convenient pocket-book format, the guide-book sold slowly. Only when the first edition had gone did climbers realize what they had missed. Second-hand prices rose swiftly and encouraged Conway to produce another edition.

But Conway had a sharp business eye. '. . . as they had been willing to pay a pound for a second-hand first edition,' he wrote, 'I decided that they should pay me the same price for a much better and fuller book, and they did.' He extended it to cover all the Pennine Alps, and it became the forerunner of a whole series of *Conway and Coolidge's Climbers' Guides*, which until quite recently were the only Alpine guide-books published in English. Despite the title, however, Conway had no hand in the production of the later volumes.

Though Conway climbed extensively in the Alps, including the Eastern Alps, he made no new ascents of any consequence. He did not have within him the sort of fire which motivated people like Mummery—his was more the questing spirit, seeking from the mountains as much in the way of aesthetic pleasure as excitement. He would climb a certain route simply because the juxtaposition of sky and rock happened to be perfect; technical difficulty didn't interest him. He was, perhaps, the greatest of all the mountain romantics, always seeking what he called 'the Perfect Place'.

Towards the end of the eighties Conway considered the possibilities of mountains other than the Alps. Short travels round the Mediterranean awakened an interest in the romance of the East, turning his thoughts to the Himalaya. He thought that here was the very region where he could find what he was seeking.

Plans were laid in 1890. Originally he considered as his companions D. W. Freshfield and A. F. Mummery, but the former withdrew and Mummery, after a trial period in the Alps, realized that his ideas on climbing were so at variance with those of Conway that a partnership would prove futile. Conway must have been very disappointed because he held Mummery in high regard.

The expedition was eventually arranged for 1892 and the area chosen was the remote Karakorum. Very little was known about the region, no mountains had been climbed there, so Conway had an open field of exploration.

The party consisted of Conway, Roudebush, McCormick, Eckenstein and young Lieutenant Bruce with his Gurkhas. The unruly Eckenstein soon left them, but the party did valuable work untangling the complicated topography of the Hispar and Baltoro Glaciers; previously unknown to Europeans. The climax was the ascent of Pioneer Peak (22,600 feet) the highest summit ever attained at that time.

The expedition was hailed as a huge success, which indeed it was, but it failed to satisfy Conway.

During this period the Alpine world was ravaged by one of its periodical controversies. Two schools of thought had arisen as to how an Alpine holiday should be spent—whether in fact a climber should stay in one convenient centre such as Chamonix or Zermatt and climb the peaks round about (a centrist, he was called) or whether he should wander from valley to valley, crossing high cols and taversing peaks (an ex-centrist). Conway was very much in favour of the latter and to prove his point he traversed the Alps from end to end in 1894. With his favourite guide, Matthias Zurbriggen, and two Gurkhas whom he had brought back from India, he crossed twenty-one peaks and thirty-nine passes in a three-months' journey extending from the Col de la Tenda in the west to the Gross Glockner in the east.

It was a glorious gesture against over-specialization, a grand appeal to the mysterious romance of the mountain world, but it was a dying cause. The increasing difficulty and technical nature of new climbs made centralization a necessity. Only in the Austrian Tyrol, which has a particularly well organized and numerous system of huts, is Conway's sort of climbing holiday carried on to any great extent nowadays.

Even his prodigious walk through the Alps failed to satisfy Conway. A winter's day in Hyde Park, when everything was white with frost and ice, convinced him that the Arctic was the place he was looking for. In 1896 and 1897 he paid two visits to Spitzbergen; on the first occasion crossing the main island and on the second climbing the barren mountains. When he had finished, Spitzbergen was no longer a blank on the map.

The following year found him in the Bolivian Andes on a long tour of exploration which included the first ascent of Illimani (20,496 feet) and the second of Aconcagua (23,080 feet). He also visited the remote island of Tierra del Fuego, where he tried in vain to climb the utterly remote and bleak Mt. Sarmiento.

In 1901, at the age of 45, Martin Conway suddenly bade farewell to mountaineering. His last 'official' climb was to lead his daughter up the Breithorn: her first climb as it had been his twenty-nine years earlier. From then on he climbed rarely, and solely for pleasure.

By this time, of course, Conway was an important public figure. He became an M.P. and Director-General of the Imperial War Museum. He was Vice-President of the Royal Geographical Society and the Society of Antiquaries. His books were very popular and whatever spare time he could find he devoted to art and to the restoration of Allington Castle, his home near Maidstone. He was the recipient of many honours, eventually becoming Lord Conway of Allington in 1931.

His sudden abandoning of exploration, his amazing switch from the wild corners of the globe to the lush homeliness of Kent, represents perhaps a re-thinking of the 'Perfect Place' he sought for so long. He died in 1937.

OSCAR ECKENSTEIN

(1859 – 1921)

OPEN ANY BOOK dealing with the early days of British rock-climbing or exploration in the Himalaya and it is almost certain that somewhere in its pages you will encounter a fleeting reference to Oscar Eckenstein. He flits in and out of the pioneering picture like some dark, unhappy, familiar, haunting Pen y Pass, hob-nobbing with the great names of the day such as Archer Thomson or Martin Conway, himself a background figure of small account. And yet, in this present age when climbing is more akin to technology than art, it is to Eckenstein that we should look as one of the important founders of the sport. He was the man who first applied technological principles to the climbing of mountains.

Oscar Johannes Ludwig Eckenstein was born in London on September 9, 1859, the son of a German father and English mother. His father had fled Germany in 1848, the year of revolutions, because he was a prominent Socialist and as such marked for the firing squad. His children—there were two girls as well as Oscar—all exhibited strong individualism, high intellects and argumentative natures. As a family they seem to have been comfortably placed, though not wealthy.

Oscar was educated at University College School from where he went on to study chemistry at London and Bonn. His interest in science, however, went far beyond his own subject and he took special interest in the realms of engineering and mathematics as they affected everyday problems.

Despite his considerable intellectual powers, which impressed everybody he met, Eckenstein made no outstanding contributions to science. In fact he held down a perfectly ordinary job connected with railway engineering. It was a terrible waste of talent but quite in keeping with his character; Oscar Eckenstein was a man utterly without ambition of any sort. He seems to have inherited some of his father's revolutionary tendencies— certainly he was in perpetual revolt against the well ordered Victorian society of his day, though he lacked the moral fibre to do anything about it.

He was in many ways the prototype of the intellectual rebels one hears so much about today. Like them he dressed shabbily, wore sandals even in town and affected a beard of Marxian proportions. On his head he wore a sort of peaked sailor-cap and he smoked a curly pipe which rivalled that of Sherlock Holmes. When he drank tea it was from a huge mug, and when he expressed an opinion, which was frequently, he did so as though any contradiction was ridiculous. He was strongly anti-British in an age of Imperialism.

In the mountains Eckenstein was tolerated because of his sincerity and ability, but he was hardly a drawing-room asset. Many people frankly disliked him though he made few real enemies. One of his friends was George Abraham, but George's relatives put their foot down when George wanted to join Eckenstein's Himalayan expedition.

Nothing is known about Eckenstein's early climbing though he seems to have been interested in mountains from boyhood. He first appears in the Alps in 1886, when he made several ascents in the Mischabel group with August Lorria, one half of the notorious Lammer and Lorria partnership who were early propagandists of the do-or-die school of climbing.

One thing emerged from his partnership with Lorria—he learned the true value of crampons for climbing ice. He wrote: *Like most British climbers, I have always scorned the use of these invaluable articles, a scorn which was entirely based on ignorance and prejudice. However, I have learnt better.* . . . Unfortunately, very few climbers heeded his advice, and he only succeeded in angering the traditionalists. There was a pathological antipathy to the use of crampons by British climbers which lasted almost up to the last war.

Not that Eckenstein bothered what others thought about him, particularly members of the Alpine Club. Since the Club represented the Establishment he was wholeheartedly 'agin' it, though he often climbed with its leading members. Instead, he set his inventive mind the task of improving existing crampons (the use of which goes back into antiquity). The result was the Eckenstein ten-point crampons, upon which all modern crampons are based.

Eckenstein claimed that because of crampons he never cut more than twenty steps in his whole career, which sounds an exaggeration but could be true. Certainly he found no need for the ponderous guides' axe which was then in fashion so he designed a short, lightweight ice-axe of his own. When Karl Blodig first saw this new axe he laughed outright and declared its inventor quite mad, but when he tried it out he quickly became convinced of its superiority. The fashion of the short ice-axe had come to stay, though even Eckenstein would have been surprised if he could have foreseen how short the modern axe was to become!

Despite the technical improvements which he made to equipment Eckenstein lacked the drive to put them to a proper test. He made no great ice climbs—in fact, no great climbs at all—his chief contribution to those stirring times being a stone-bombarded route up the south-west face of the Dom (led by Alexander Burgener) and a new route on the Dent Blanche described by the *Alpine Journal* as 'believed to be the worst yet taken'.

In 1892 Eckenstein was invited to take part in Conway's Karakorum expedition, the first of its kind. Conway's motive seems to have been that he wanted a scientist to accompany the expedition for prestige purposes, but why he picked on Eckenstein is beyond comprehension. Their outlooks on climbing, and one would imagine, most other things, were so at variance that trouble was inevitable. Eckenstein soon quit the party.

Although Alpine huts were becoming commonplace during the last few years of the century, an individualist like Eckenstein preferred the pleasures of camping. In 1898 Karl Blodig came across him camped on the Schönbiel Glacier. The tent was

THE BRENVA FACE OF MONT BLANC · In the centre is the ice arête of the Old Brenva route beyond which lies the Route Major and Sentinelle.

MONTE ROSA · Lyskamm on the right. The Cresta Rey can be seen as a thin dark ridge rising to the summit of Monte Rosa from the glacier basin.

THE EIGER · The great *nordwand* is in shadow. Lauper's route lies up the buttresses and snow just left of this.

equipped with a rubber underlay and a cork mattress (anticipating sleeping mats by fifty years) and Eckenstein had fresh meat and poultry which he kept wholesome by using a crevasse as a deep freeze.

It was about this time that Eckenstein first met Alasteir Crowley, with whom he formed a lasting friendship. Crowley was a strange man, evil. He practised unholy rites and black magic and he called himself the Great Beast. A considerable number of influential people came under Crowley's spell, for he had a magnetic personality, but Eckenstein was not one of them. He never ceased to pour scorn on Crowley's 'magic', but for some strange reason the friendship continued, and Crowley regarded Eckenstein as a kind of superman. Indeed, of all the people whom Crowley ever knew Eckenstein was the only one for whom he had nothing but admiration. All the same, his association with the abominable Crowley tore to shreds what little remained of Eckenstein's reputation.

Crowley was also a climber—there is a route which bears his name on Napes Needle—and in 1900 he and Eckenstein visited Mexico together, making an ascent of Popacatapetl. They also tried to climb an active volcano called Colima, only turning back when the hot ashes had burnt through the soles of their boots!

Two years later Eckenstein organized an international expedition to attempt K2, the second highest mountain in the world, and he made Crowley his second-in-command. The other members were Guy Knowles, two Austrians called Pfannl and Wesseley, and the Swiss doctor Jacot-Guillarmot. Despite bad weather dogging the expedition, it did invaluable survey work on the glaciers, and Guillarmot and Wesseley reached a height of 21,400 feet on the north-east ridge of the mountain.

The expedition was not without its comic-melodrama. Scarcely had they arrived in India when Eckenstein was arrested as a spy, some say as the result of behind-the-scenes pressure on the authorities by Martin Conway, who had never forgiven Eckenstein for what had happened ten years previously, and who also had no desire for the K2 expedition to outshine his own. Eckenstein only managed to continue after a personal interview with the Viceroy.

Crowley, too, as one could imagine, contributed to the fun and games. On one occasion some heavily laden porters refused to cross a steep snow slope which overhung an enormous precipice, understandably afraid that they might slide off to their doom. Crowley showed them that it was perfectly safe. With a great leap he sprang down the slope and went sliding towards the cliff, pulling himself up short a few feet from the edge. His European companions thought him quite mad—but the porters crossed the slope.

However, the volatile Crowley had no place on an expedition. The whole affair ended when he had a violent disagreement with Knowles and chased him off the mountain at pistol point!

As an original member of the Climbers' Club, Eckenstein was one of the founders of Welsh climbing. With J. M. A. Thomson he pioneered the first routes on Lliwedd, then regarded as the experts' cliff. Thomson led in every instance and in fact Eckenstein very rarely led anywhere; even in the Alps he generally employed a guide.

In tackling the open faces of Lliwedd, Thomson was putting into practice the principles that Eckenstein was preaching— that climbing was essentially a matter of balance and that if holds were properly used they need not be big or incut. It was simply a matter of stresses properly applied.

Nothing of technical interest to climbing escaped Eckenstein's attention. He was the first to point out which knots were strongest, and the increased strength to be gained by tying them with the lay of the rope. He also investigated the sharp-edged tricouni nails when they first made their appearance, and which many climbers favoured until the rubber sole came into use after the last war.

Eckenstein can never be classed as a great climber like Young or Mummery, but he made his own unique contributions to the sport. Eccentric, brilliant, uncouth—a rough diamond, as Longstaff once described him. He died of consumption in 1921.

JOHN NORMAN COLLIE

(1859 – 1942)

ONE DAY IN the year 1886 a young fisherman stood by a burn in the Isle of Skye, watching with fascination the antics of two alpinists on the steep rocks of Sgurr nan Gillean. He had never seen anything like it before.

Hundreds of feet above me, on what appeared to be rocks as steep as the walls of a house, they moved slowly backwards and forwards, but always getting higher, till they finally reached the summit. I knew nothing about climbing and it seemed to me perfectly marvellous that human beings should be able to do such things.

So wrote the young Norman Collie, then science tutor at Cheltenham Ladies' College, and on the threshold of a brilliant scientific career. He determined there and then to try this fascinating sport of climbing for himself.

John Norman Collie was born in 1859, the son of an Aberdeen business man. When Norman was 6 his father retired and took a shooting at Glassel on Deeside, where the family remained for five years. During this period young Collie was educated by private tutors, but he had plenty of opportunity to explore the countryside around his home, soon becoming an expert on all branches of nature lore. He later claimed that the years spent on Deeside had a great effect on his attitude to life.

This happy period soon ended. The family moved to Bristol and Norman entered Charterhouse, only to leave again when the family fortunes took a downwards turn. He went instead as a day boy to Clifton College, but he was such a poor pupil that he was expelled and it was not until he shook off the arid dust of the classics to take up science at the University College of Bristol that his true genius began to show. He took a Ph.D. at Wurtzburg and was appointed to his job in Cheltenham—a post he disliked intensely. Finally he was made the first Professor of

Organic Chemistry at University College, London, where he stayed until his retirement in 1928.

Every field of science interested Collie. He was one of the first to investigate the effect of electric discharge through gases, and it is largely owing to his work with the rare gas neon that we now have the familiar neon signs. His original thinking, combined with his interest in photography, was demonstrated when a hospital sent a woman patient to him who was reputed to have a needle point embedded in her thumb. Collie placed the thumb on a photographic plate and exposed it to the recently discovered Röntgen rays. The developed plate showed the exact position of the needle. It was the first medical use of X-ray photography.

Collie was a good teacher, somewhat given to sarcasm. He was known to his students as the Old Man, a title of which he was inordinately proud. To his contemporaries he seemed something of a recluse: a bachelor who lived in rooms lavishly decorated with oriental art treasures and stacked with piles of books which sometimes reached to the ceiling. His impeccable tastes in wine and cigars, his exquisite food, were famous, and he frequently entertained distinguished gatherings of eminent scientists and explorers.

He was an inveterate smoker. The story is told of how on a difficult climb one day his two companions carried on a loud conversation about the bad effects of tobacco on fitness, obviously intending Collie to overhear it. He said nothing, but whenever he had a particularly difficult pitch to lead during the rest of the climb, he ostentatiously took out his pipe, lit it, and climbed with it in his mouth.

In appearance he was lean, erect, with pale sunken features, sombre eyes, and hair which hung lank and greying. He looked for all the world like the pictures of Sherlock Holmes which were just appearing in the *Strand Magazine* at the time.

Though he had many good friends, he did not make acquaintance easily. One day a stranger tried to strike up conversation in the lounge of the Sligachan Inn in Skye. Fixing on some photographs of the surrounding mountains which decorated the walls he asked:

'Have you been up any of these mountains?'

'Yes,' said Collie. Then silence.

'Have you been up that one?' Pointing to a picture.

'Yes.'

'And that one?' Another picture, more imposing.

'Yes.'

'And that?'

'Yes.'

The man rose, his face full of disbelief. 'What are you,' he flung back, as he left the room, 'a ruddy steeplejack?'

Though he gained high academic distinction Collie would have been the first to admit that science was only a part of his life and a lesser part at that. From the moment he saw Stocker and Parker on Sgurr nan Gillean in 1886, his first love was the mountains, and those of Skye in particular.

At that time Skye was very little visited by climbers. Only the Pilkingtons had climbed there at all extensively and many of the peaks were virgin. Collie rectified this. In 1887 and 1888, with a local man, John MacKenzie, as guide, he climbed every summit in the Cuillins except Sgurr Coire an Lochain. Mac-Kenzie led many of the climbs and it seems likely that it was from him Collie learnt rudimentary rock-climbing technique. They remained firm friends until MacKenzie's death in the thirties.

In 1890 they began a systematic survey of the Cuillin ridge because of the unreliability of the Ordnance Survey. Each has a peak named after him—Sgurr MhicCoinnich (MacKenzie's Peak) and Sgurr Thormaid (Norman's Peak).

Though Skye always remained his first love, Collie began to explore further afield. In 1892 he was at Chamonix and became one of that immortal quartet—Mummery, Slingsby, Collie and Hastings—who put modern climbing on its feet. It was Collie who gave the name Dent du Requin, meaning Shark's Tooth, to an unnamed aiguille which has since become one of the most popular in the area.

Nearer home he visited the Lake District, where he created a mild sensation by leading Moss Ghyll on Scafell, a steep gully then regarded as one of the great unsolved problems.

During the ascent of Moss Ghyll Collie used his ice-axe to chop a step in an apparently holdless slab. To the purists this was a terrible crime—defacing the rock to make the climb easier —but Collie didn't seem to mind. He had something of an imp in his character at times, which made him take great delight in stirring controversy. But even the purists climbed the gully with the aid of the hold which Collie so conveniently cut, and the 'Collie Step' became part of climbing lore.

During the Easter of 1894 Collie, with J. Collier, G. A. Solly, and later Geoffrey Hastings—a very strong team—made a concentrated attack on the crags of the Scottish mainland, which had been totally neglected up till that date. They made the first route ever done on the fine precipice of Buachaille Etive Mor (Collie's Climb) in Glencoe, and the first ascent of Tower Ridge on Ben Nevis, which Collie compared favourably with the Italian Ridge of the Matterhorn. This campaign drew attention to the tremendous potential of the Scottish crags and was the start of serious rock-climbing in Scotland.

Meanwhile, Skye was not forgotten. In 1891, with Mac-Kenzie and King, Collie made the first crossing of the notorious Thearlaich-Dubh Gap, a savage gash in the ridge which prevented climbers from making a traverse. He also climbed Sgurr Coire an Lochain, the last unclimbed summit in Britain.

Besides his Alpine climbs Collie also visited the Canadian Rockies and the remote Lofoten Islands. In 1895 he joined Mummery and Hastings on the ill-fated attempt to climb Nanga Parbat in the Himalaya. They really had very little idea of the enormous task they had undertaken but they made some valiant attempts to climb a mountain which was far too difficult for them.

In the final stages of the expedition Mummery lost his life trying to cross an unknown pass and this so affected Collie that he refused to discuss it for the rest of his life. In his book, *Climbing on the Himalaya,* Collie gives a moving picture of the frantic search which he and Hastings made for their lost friend, and the growing realization of the inevitable tragedy.

Mummery was only the first of many such victims that Nanga Parbat was to claim before the German mountaineer, Hermann Buhl, reached the summit in 1953.

In 1899 Collie returned to Skye to make his notable discovery, the famous Cioch at Sron na Ciche. Returning from a climb one evening he was passing the great slabs of the Sron na Ciche when his attention was attracted to a strange shadow cast upon them. His logical mind made him realize that the shadow must be caused by some large rock protuberance, but since he had no time to investigate it, he could do no more than take a photograph.

Unfortunately, he was not able to return to the Sron na Ciche for seven years. When he did, he and MacKenzie made their way up the enormous slabs to discover that the shadow was caused by a curious tower of rock, jutting 50 feet out from the cliff. He called it the Cioch, and it has been popular with climbers ever since.

Collie's life was one continual adventure. Despite his scientific upbringing he claimed to have seen the Grey Man of Ben Macdhui, a ghost which is supposed to haunt that Cairngorm summit. It is quite possible that he was just having a little fun at public expense—his story received a lot of attention and still comes in for frequent discussion amongst climbers—but on the other hand there is no doubt that he refused to go near Ben Macdhui again!

In the opinion of Geoffrey Winthrop Young, Collie and Slingsby were the two finest mountaineers of their generation. Of Collie he wrote: *Of all the wholehearted mountaineers I have known, Collie alone remained to the end wholly and passionately absorbed in the mountain world.*

Collie retired to Sligachan in Skye where he died on November 1, 1942, at the age of 84. By his own wish he was buried in Struan churchyard next to his lifelong companion, John MacKenzie, in the shadow of his beloved Cuillins.

GUIDO REY

(1861 – 1935)

GUIDO REY WAS born in Turin on October 20, 1861, the son of a wealthy industrialist. He was related to the influential Sella family who played a part not only in the formation of the Italian Alpine Club, but in the foundation of Italy itself as a unified state under King Victor Emmanuel. Young Guido was brought up in an atmosphere of mountaineering and fiery patriotism which gave him a romantic outlook scarcely ever equalled amongst mountaineers.

As a young man he climbed guideless with some of the best Italian climbers of the day—men such as Fiorio, Ratti, and Vaccarone. He made some notable ascents during this time, including the first ascent of Ciamarella from the south, the south ridge of Lyskamm, and routes on the Aiguille d'Arves and Monte Viso. His notes on the last two incurred the displeasure of no less an authority than Coolidge, self-appointed guardian of everything to do with the Alps, but young Rey stuck to his guns and refused to be bullied by the cantankerous old lion.

This youthful period of adventure came to an end when Rey's younger brother was killed in an accident near the Col du Géant. From then on Rey climbed only with guides, and his wealth and position assured him of the best, such as Castagneri and the Maquignaz family.

For Rey, his guides were like knights in shining armour. He hardly saw them as normal human beings and he endowed them with powers which even the best did not possess. The climbing of some great mountain was to him like St. George slaying the dragon.

Despite his guides Rey never made a major first ascent. His two most original contributions were the crossing of the Colle Gnifetti from Macugnaga, and the first ascent of the Pointe

Blanche on the east ridge of the Dent d'Héréns. If only he had followed the entire east ridge as Ryan did later, he would have made the finest ascent of his career.

In 1886 Rey made the third ascent of the south-south-west ridge of the Dufourspitze on Monte Rosa; a beautiful line leading directly to the summit from the Grenz Glacier and known thereafter as the *Cresta Rey*—though in fact it had first been climbed twelve years earlier by Eustace Hulton. It must be added, however, that Rey himself was not responsible for his name being given to the climb.

As a contributor to climbing journals Rey showed himself to be prolific, sophisticated and highly literate. He could read Latin and English as fluently as his native Italian. His outlook on the mountains was greatly influenced by the works written by the English pioneers, such as Whymper and Stephen; he had an almost frightening respect for the English—there was something in their reserve and solidity which appealed to his Latin temperament. Whymper, whom he once met by accident near the Matterhorn, he regarded as a demi-god.

In 1890 Rey first tried to climb the Furggen Ridge of the Matterhorn, which was then still virgin. It was the last of the mountain's great ridges to remain unclimbed and Rey, for whom the Matterhorn was the supreme mountain, was determined to succeed. But what chance did he stand? Where the great Mummery had failed, and where Ryan and Young were to fail as well, what hope was there for Guido Rey, even though he was backed by the élite of the Valtournanche guides?

He soon found that the climbing was much too difficult for him and he gave up his attempts hoping that someone else might come along and do the climb. Every time he looked at the Furggen Ridge it seemed to mock him. For nine years he waited in vain, then, patience at an end, he returned to the attack.

And attack is the right word, for Rey's attempts on the Furggen Ridge were like military manœuvres. Gathering together practically every guide in the Valtournanche he sent part of his forces up the Italian Ridge whilst he, with the rest,

4*

climbed the Furggen as far as the final shoulder. This in itself was not particularly difficult—the hard part of the ridge is the final wall which shows up so well on photographs of the mountain.

Rey reached the foot of the steep wall and the men who had climbed the other ridge reached the top of the wall by a simple descent. The idea was to employ what climbers call top-rope tactics—that is, those on top of the wall lowered a rope and with its security around them those below tried to climb the cliff. But the wall was overhanging. Time and again Rey and his men went at it, climbed a few feet, then peeled off and hung spiralling in mid-air until their companions lowered them back to the ledge below the wall. Defeated once again, Rey ordered his little army to retreat.

Rey was now so obsessed with the idea of beating the obstinate ridge into submission that he had no intention of giving up so easily. Four days later he was back again, he and his guides ascending the Italian Ridge and scrambling down to the top of the great Furggen wall. The guides drove iron stakes into the rock and from these lowered a long rope ladder. Rey descended the ladder and then climbed back up it, and thus the Furggen was 'conquered'.

Of course, the whole thing was nothing more than a symbolic gesture on Rey's part—the whim of a rich romantic unwilling to give the mountain best. The Furggen ridge was not climbed properly until 1911, and then only by a devious route which wasn't improved until 1930. The direct route, straight up the formidable final wall, was not accomplished until 1941 and is still reckoned one of the most difficult ridges in the Alps.

In 1904 Rey published his great work *Il Monte Cervino* (*The Matterhorn*) which was translated into French, German and English and is still the definitive book on the early history of the mountain. In it he told of his own climbs and he also revealed for the first time details of the correspondence between Quintino Sella and Felice Giordano concerning the Italian attempt of 1865—the famous intrigue which had caused Whymper to cry 'Treachery!' and rush off on his own ill-fated attempt.

He followed this in 1914 with *Alpinismo Acrobatico*, relating his experiences in the Chamonix Aiguilles and the Dolomites. In England it appeared under the less sensational title of *Peaks and Precipices*.

His writings revealed not only a romantic but also one of the true mountain philosophers; a man who knew what it was all about and could put it into words. About accidents caused by over-ambitious climbers he said: 'We go to the mountains to live and not to die.' He also warned about regarding climbing simply as an extension to the gymnasium: 'There is in mountaineering something more than vain ambition to climb difficult peaks, there is *soul*.'

Though he was 53 years old when the Great War broke out Rey at once volunteered his services and managed to reach the front line, but he was involved in a motor accident which put paid to his military career, and in the end to his climbing as well.

He spent his summers at the Villa Rey, which he built near Breuil, in the shadow of the Matterhorn. He would spend hours just gazing at the mountain, or watching climbers through his powerful telescope. Though he deplored the coming of the motor road up the valley, he kept open house for any climbers who cared to call, and he was seldom without company, either distinguished foreign mountaineers or simply Italian boys and girls out on a mountain holiday. Rey did a lot in his lifetime to encourage outdoor pursuits among young people.

Though Rey could never be counted amongst the truly great mountaineers—he lacked the fire for that—it is true to say that when he died in June 1935 mountaineering lost one of the best friends it has ever had.

CHARLES GRANVILLE BRUCE

(1866 – 1939)

THE NAME OF General Bruce is popularly linked with the great pre-war expeditions to Everest—enormous caravans of porters crossing the bleak Tibetan plateau, the staunchly public-school climbers with lots of courage and precious little else, and Base Camps stocked with good food and champagne.

But Bruce was much more than this; more than a retired General commanding a mountaineering army. He was a larger than life-sized character whose presence commanded respect all along the Frontier, whose bellowing laugh had roared in most of the Himalayan valleys, and whose jokes were repeated in in every bazaar from Kandahar to Darjeeling. Big, brave, tough and devil-may-care, he revelled in the nickname of Old Bruiser.

He came of autocratic parentage and as time went on he collected enough decorations and honours to fill a couple of lines of this page.

He was commissioned in the Oxfordshire Light Infantry at the age of 21, but two years later he opted for service in the Indian Army and was gazetted to the 5th Gurkha Rifles. This was an extremely happy chance, as it turned out, because it was Bruce's association with Gurkhas which was to have a profound effect on Himalayan mountaineering.

He began climbing on the small peaks bordering Kashmir in 1890, his aim being to train troops in hill warfare. His tough little men soon showed that they were natural climbers and he sent one of his favourite N.C.O.s, Subadar Major Harkabir Thapa, to the Russian Pamirs with Colonel Stewart. It was a time when the boundaries between Indian and Russian territories were not clearly defined and any travel in the region was dangerous. Harkabir so distinguished himself that he was awarded the Indian Order of Merit, which is roughly equivalent to the V.C.

Bruce could already see that the 5th was rapidly becoming an élite mountain corps, and the following years proved how effective such a body of men could be. During the 'nineties the Frontier was the scene of one bloody rebellion after another as local despots rose against the Raj, and the 5th fought in every campaign. The army authorities were, for once, alive to the value of this new kind of soldier, whom they began calling 'mountain scouts' and they raised the numbers from 150 to 600, gave them the latest Lee Enfield rifles and even allowed them to cut their trousers off at the knees as Bruce suggested —the first time that 'shorts' were allowed in the British Army.

About his own part in the desperate frontier campaigns Bruce was very reticent. Once, when a well-meaning lady asked him about his adventures he replied, 'I think I have run away from every Pathan tribe on the Frontier at one time or another!'

Between campaigns Bruce continued training his men in hill-craft and several of them became good mountaineers in their own right. Harkabir, for example, once made a daring solo ascent of an unknown 16,700-ft. peak simply for the enjoyment of it. In those days particularly, and to a certain extent even today, this sort of attitude on the part of a native is remarkable because climbing for pleasure is a pastime usually reserved for nations which are prosperous and have plenty of leisure.

Some of the tactics the Gurkhas used were drastic. On one occasion the need arose for some porters to descend a steep ice slope of about a 100 feet. Bruce cut steps down the first 50 feet then he fashioned a huge platform in the ice. The porters came down one at a time and Harkabir made them sit on the platform. A quick shove and they went sliding down the remaining 50 feet at considerable velocity into the waiting arms of Bruce! After the initial shock wore off the porters thought it a huge joke—they wanted to climb back up for another go!

In 1892 came Bruce's big chance to demonstrate the ability of his men and his own knowledge of the Himalaya when he was asked to join Conway's great Karakorum Expedition. They climbed Pioneer Peak (22,600 feet) and Conway returned home in a blaze of glory, but it would not have happened without the excellent work of Bruce and his men.

Bruce was a master of the native tongues. He spoke most of the Frontier dialects and could laugh and joke with his men in their own language, which gave him an enormous advantage in popularity. He also understood the native names for mountains and regarded them as the proper ones—he had no time for the re-naming of peaks with European names, which was then popular with certain explorers.

Conway was one of these, and Bruce was delighted when one day he discovered a mountain with the impossible name of Boiyohaghurdooanashur. He went straight-faced to Conway with the proposal that it should be at once re-named Mount John Jones Jenkins. But Conway was sharp enough to recognize when his leg was being pulled: 'He got rather fussy,' Bruce recalled later. The idea was dropped.

In the winter of that same year Bruce was fighting in Chilas when he saw Nanga Parbat for the first time and was very impressed. Later he joined the famous Colonel Younghusband on a mission to Chitral and the two of them climbed the shapely Ispero Zorn.

1895 saw the fateful expedition to Nanga Parbat of Mummery, Collie, and Hastings, and Bruce joined them with two of his men, Goman Singh and Raghobir. They spent a fearfully cold night in trying to cross a spur of the Nanga Parbat range, and shortly after this Bruce had to return to barracks for medical treatment. He was suffering from suppressed mumps and in considerable pain.

However, he left behind his two men and it was Raghobir who accompanied Mummery on the Diamiri ribs when Collie fell ill. The climbing was stupendous for such high altitudes— probably as technically difficult as any high-altitude rock climbing has ever been. It was abandoned when Raghobir, too, became ill.

Unfortunately, both the Gurkhas vanished with Mummery

when he attempted to cross from the Diamai to the Rakhiot valley by an unknown snow pass, and like Mummery, were never found.

Bruce and his Gurkhas were becoming well known to mountaineers. He had taken them to the Alps and even Skye—one of them, Karbir, was with Conway when the latter traversed the Alps from end to end in 1894.

In 1898 Bruce made a recce of the Nun Kun mountains in the Punjab, then very incorrectly shown on the maps. With him went a brother officer, Major F. G. Lucas and two experienced Gurkhas, Karbir and Harkabir. The supply details make interesting reading—Bruce, Lucas and Bruce's wife, sixteen Gurkhas, seven servants, five ponies, two or three yaks, fifty to sixty coolies and a small flock of sheep!

They carried out a preliminary survey and at the same time gave the Gurkhas training, since most of them were new recruits. It was sometimes hectic: 'no easy matter,' wrote Bruce, 'with fourteen new men, all very active, and most of them very careless and given to larking in dangerous places.'

In 1907 Bruce, with Longstaff and Mumm, obtained permission to attempt Mount Everest, but at the last moment the India Office withdrew it on political grounds. Instead the party went to Nanda Devi, and though they did not succeed in penetrating the formidable defences of that big mountain they did climb Trisul (23,360 feet). They also reconnoitred the Kamet area and the five months which they spent in the Himalaya laid down the foundation which enabled later climbers to meet with success.

By this time Bruce was 42 years old, but fitter and more active than many a man only half his age. His extraordinary zest for life remained unbounded—he would wrestle, ride or shoot with any man who cared to challenge him. He was now in charge of his regiment and it must have surprised many a young subaltern coming out fresh from England to discover the Colonel having a free-for-all on the barrack square with half a dozen of his soldiers! He was a prodigious load-carrier, like 'a steam engine plus goods train' as Conway put it, and whenever he was confined to regimental duties he would keep fit by making a daily run up a nearby hill, *carrying his batman*.

He loved practical jokes and would keep his men in constant fits of laughter with tricks played on them. He could also, when occasion demanded, swear for minutes on end without repeating himself—a feat which Tom Longstaff said 'had me transfixed with envy'.

During the First World War Bruce and his men saw action in Gallipoli. Unfortunately he received a severe head wound and had to be invalided home to England. The War Office were very concerned at this loss, for Bruce had such an effect on those under him that his presence was reckoned to be equivalent to another battalion. His men would have followed him to Hell and back.

After the war came the Everest expeditions, but Bruce was by this time almost 60 and strictly a non-playing captain. What he had to contribute was an unrivalled knowledge of the country and its peoples, both sorely needed in those days when both Nepal and Tibet were lands normally forbidden to foreigners.

It was Bruce who suggested that the peaceful cousin of the Gurkha, called the Sherpa, might make a useful man for high altitude climbing, and how right he was has been proved time and again. It was Sherpa Tensing who reached the summit of Everest in 1953 along with Edmund Hillary.

Charlie Bruce died in July 1939. He had impressive obituaries in all the leading newspapers and journals, but nowhere was he mourned more deeply than the remote valleys of Nepal.

OWEN GLYNNE JONES

(1867 – 1899)

EARLY IN THE summer of 1888 a young Londoner had a
hair-raising experience on Cader Idris in Wales. He had walked
up to the mountain from Barmouth, where he often holidayed
with his family, and his attention had been attracted by a long
jagged spine of rock which reminded him forcibly of those
splendid illustrations he had seen in books about Alpine climbing. He had read many Alpine books and was filled with ambition to try his hand at Alpine climbing, but what could an
impecunious student do? Suddenly, on Cader Idris, he found a
substitute.

He had no companions, no rope, no nails in his boots even.
He also had no idea how to climb rocks and as the rotten bits
of Cader Idris crashed away on either side of his ridge, to go
plunging down into deep cwms, he must often have wished he
had never set out on such a fool's errand. Yet he managed to
reach the top safely—his first climb, and incidentally, the
first ascent of the Cyfrwy Arête.

Owen Glynne Jones was born in 1867 the son of a carpenter
and builder who had left his native Wales to seek success in
Paddington. The boy was gifted both physically and mentally.
He was as strong as an ox—he once did a single-handed pull-
up to a beam, carrying George Abraham under his other arm.
He graduated from Finsbury Technical College and became
an assistant lecturer at the Central Institution. Later he was
appointed to the City of London School where he established
science on the curriculum and where he spent the remainder of
his working life.

Jones's adventure on Cader Idris was an isolated example of
youthful spirit rather than the start of his climbing career. He
knew no climbers personally and he did not realize that the

sport was practised on our own mountains as well as the Alps. Not until two years later—the Easter of 1890—did he visit Wasdale Head, where he met an alpinist called W. M. Crook who took him climbing on Pillar. Jones was flattered by Crook's invitation and Crook was equally impressed by the powerful lead of his new acquaintance.

Later that year, as he was walking down the Strand, Jones's eye fell on a photograph of Napes Needle displayed in a shop window. He had no idea such rocks existed at Wasdale—a perfect Alpine gendarme! He could scarcely wait until he had a chance to scale the pinnacle.

According to Norman Collie, Jones returned to the Lakes in the autumn of 1890 and tried to scale the Needle solo, but got stuck. Fortunately, Collie was on hand to effect his rescue. Jones himself, however, claimed that his first acquaintance with the Needle was during the Easter of the following year, when he climbed it with a colleague from the Central Institution, Dr. W. E. Sumpner.

Napes Needle stands on a side of Great Gable and is part of a system of steep ridges which are popular with climbers. It is a broad based pinnacle, rising to a shoulder, after which it tapers considerably—about 60 feet high in all. Jones climbed solo to the shoulder (he had rushed ahead) and Sumpner threw up one end of the rope to him then tied himself on the other end. When he had reached Jones they inspected the slender top block. To reach it, a delicate press-up, or mantelshelf, was necessary, on to a tiny ledge and Jones asked Sumpner for a shoulder to steady himself. So began the usual way of climbing Napes Needle, though nowadays modern experts have climbed it in a variety of ways.

It was during this holiday that Jones was invited by Dr. C. G. Munro to join him in the Alps. It seemed to Jones that every ambition had been realized. At last he was to get to grips with the real mountains!

Yet it is strange that a man can often strive after one ambition and yet acquire fame for something quite different. Jones is a case in point. He ardently desired to make a name for himself as an Alpinist, and he climbed practically all the big peaks, but the only expedition that was out of the ordinary was a winter ascent of the Schreckhorn in 1897. His English rock-climbing came to him so naturally that he thought very little of it—and yet it is this for which he is remembered.

During the eight years in which he was a visitor to Wasdale Head Jones assumed a supremacy which was never challenged by any of his contemporaries. He came into the sport knowing nothing about it, and he left it firmly set on the traditional lines as we know it today.

Jones was not always an easy man to get along with. Casual acquaintances found him brusque and off-hand in his manner. This may explain why he climbed so much alone until the sheer force of his ability made others seek him out as a companion.

On one of his solo exploits he was almost killed. In the January of 1893 he attempted to climb Moss Ghyll on Scafell, when the mountain was coated with a layer of powder snow. The climb was then regarded as a very serious one—the first ascent had taken place only a few months previously—and sure enough, Jones fell off at the Collie Step. Fortunately for him he had arranged a sort of automatic belay which held him firmly in the gully, or he would have fallen over 250 feet to the screes. As it was he suffered two cracked ribs and bruises, yet he imme-diately went at the pitch again and successfully completed the ascent. As if to gain revenge on the mountain, he repeated the climb two days later.

In the same year Jones met two of the pioneers, J. W. Robin-son and W. P. Haskett Smith. With Robinson he made the first ascent of Sergeant Crag Gully in Langstrath—a rather remote climb—and Kern Knotts Chimney on Gable. With Haskett Smith he climbed on Cader Idris and their purpose was to collect information for a guide-book which Haskett Smith was compiling. It was probably the first time that climbs had been specifically done for a guide-book, though it is ironical that of all the mountains in Wales, Cader Idris is nowadays one of the least popular.

The winter of 1895 was particularly significant for Jones

because he met for the first time the two Abraham brothers of Keswick, who were making a name for themselves as mountain photographers. Henceforth, they were his most constant companions.

It was a trio of young and forceful minds who brought to the crags a certain degree of professionalism which some climbers considered undesirable. The Abraham brothers in particular came in for some harsh comments and their pictures were criticized even to the extent of suggesting that they were actually faked by tilting the camera. The fact of the matter was that many of those who made the criticism had little or no experience of British rock-climbing and the Abrahams were breaking new ground by actually showing climbers in action.

Jones ignored the critics. He posed for the Abrahams on some of the most famous climbs of the day (they sold the pictures as postcards to tourists) and in return the Abrahams provided Jones with illustrations for his comprehensive *Rock Climbing in the English Lake District.*

When this book appeared in 1896 it did a great deal to popularize the sport. In it Jones classified climbs into four grades of difficulty: Easy, Moderate, Difficult and Exceptionally Severe. With some slight modifications this system has been in use in Britain ever since, and various attempts to introduce the Continental system which grades climbs numerically from 1 to 6 have died on the altar of tradition.

Jones did some of his best climbs about this time—C Gully on the Screes above Wastwater, Walker's Gully on Pillar Rock, and perhaps his most famous route, the short but sensational-looking Kern Knotts Crack on Gable which he led after a preliminary investigation on a top rope. On Scafell, too, he was particularly active and though he did not reach Hopkinson's Cairn he did make five new routes including the Pinnacle from Deep Ghyll and from Lord's Rake. He almost climbed what was to become Botterill's Slab, but he was stopped by icy holds.

With the help of the Abrahams, Jones was slowly evolving a safer way of climbing, which was to grow into our British system where one man moves at a time and those who are not moving are tied to the rock. In the Alps, where time is more important because the climbs are longer, this method can only be employed where the climbing is very difficult—there the method is for climbers to move together on easy rocks, and use what is called a 'direct belay' for more tricky pitches.

Jones also re-discovered Mummery's old trick of climbing delicate pitches in stockinged feet, when the damp wool of a stocking will adhere to the rock better than nails and a more sensitive balance can be achieved. As a stylist, though, he was not much to watch—'His attack was rough and spasmodic,' George Abraham used to say, and there is no doubt he saw climbing in physical terms. On pitches he knew, he could move very fast, and though he liked to compare the problems involved in climbing with those of a mathematical puzzle, he undoubtedly used his great strength to advantage. He would climb anything offering a challenge—he even got a considerable distance up Cleopatra's Needle.

During the Easter of 1899, he visited Snowdonia with the Abrahams to collect material for a sequel to his Lakeland guidebook. Whilst he was there he made three popular climbs on Tryfan—North Buttress, Terrace Wall Variant and the Milestone Buttress Ordinary Route. The last of these gained its strange name because it lay up a buttress of rock immediately opposite the tenth milestone on the road from Bangor. Because it is so easily accessible it quickly became popular and it is probably the most frequently climbed route in Britain.

For his Alpine season that year Jones chose Arolla. He made a number of the usual ascents, then he persuaded F. W. Hill to accompany him on the west ridge of the Dent Blanche, now known as the Ferpècle Arête or Jones Arête. It was not a new climb, having first been ascended ten years previously.

They spent the night of Sunday, August 27, at the little Bricolla chalets on a grassy alp below the mountain. They were five in number—Jones with his two guides, Furrer and Zurbriggen, and Hill with his guide Vuignier.

At 3 a.m. on the Monday they set off for the arête with

Furrer leading Jones's rope and Vuignier leading Hill. Once on the rocks it was obvious that the route was going to be difficult with lots of smooth slabs, but they were all good climbers and they made their way quickly but carefully upwards enjoying to the full the gloriously fine day. As soon as the difficulties had commenced Vuignier had tied on to Jones so that they became a rope of five with Hill as last man.

When they were about two hours from the summit Furrer found the way blocked by a chimney full of ice and impossible to climb. To the left of the chimney was an equally smooth wall but beyond that again lay a small rounded buttress which seemed to offer a chance. Furrer traversed across to this buttress but found to his annoyance that he could not reach suitable holds, so Zurbriggen joined him in order to place an ice axe as a sort of extra foothold. Furrer, however, found the situation precarious and he did not trust Zurbriggen to hold the axe steadily enough for balance, so Jones was also brought across to give assistance. The three men were about thirty feet to the left of Vuignier who was an equal distance away from Hill.

Suddenly Furrer, standing full stretch on the axe, toppled over backwards knocking Zurbriggen and Jones off their stance. The rope whipped out and Vuignier had no hope of saving himself before he too was plucked from the cliff. Hill clutched at a firm rock to try and take the strain he new must come, but to his great surprise the rope snapped and he saw his four companions go hurtling down the mountain to their deaths.

Hill survived because the prudent Vuignier had taken care to lay a coil of rope between Hill and himself round a spike of rock, and it was sheer bad luck that the weight of four men should come on it simultaneously—a strain no rope of those days could take.

Hill, however, was in a terrible predicament. He was badly shocked by the accident and he was alone on a desperate climb. He knew that he could never manage to descend the way they had come up and that the only possible chance of escape lay in completing the climb, solo. Incredibly, this he managed to do and then, with no food or drink, he descended the ordinary route of the mountain (itself no easy matter), survived a blizzard and two days later arrived half dead at the Stafel Alp Hotel, the nearest habitation.

Owen Glynne Jones was buried in the cemetery at Evolène in the shadow of the mountains he loved best. His most lasting memorials, however, will always be a wall of rock on the shoulder of Gable and the tenth milestone from Bangor.

EUSTACE THOMAS

(1869 – 1960)

FROM TIME TO time it falls the lot of a mountaineer to take part in a rescue, and the commonest job at such times is helping to carry the stretcher down into the valley. It is a wearisome task, even when there are plenty of volunteers, but it is made infinitely easier than it would otherwise be by the splendid design of the stretcher itself. The Thomas Stretcher, as it is called, was invented thirty years ago by a Manchester engineer and it says much for the basic design that it remains virtually unaltered today.

Few mountaineers could have a more permanently useful memorial, and yet if the stretcher was the only contribution which Thomas made to British mountaineering, there would be little story to tell. In fact, between the two World Wars, Eustace Thomas was one of the hardest 'goers' the mountains have ever known.

He was born in 1869, the son of a London Tax-collector. Educated at the City of London School, he took his degree at Finsbury Technical College, where, by one of those curious coincidences, he was a contemporary of the great Owen Glynne Jones, though unlike Jones, Thomas at that time had no interest in mountains.

That came later and in an unusual way. It stemmed from a move he made to Manchester in 1900 to join his brother in an electrical engineering business, when, to keep fit, he began to play golf (at which he was very good) and to take up road walking. He was already in his thirties—rather late, some might think, to begin energetic pursuits.

Now it so happens that the senior mountaineering club of the Manchester area is the Rucksack Club, which has always been a haven for strong walkers and in 1909 Thomas was per-

suaded to join their ranks. This introduced him to the high
moors of the Peak District, bleak and very rough under foot,
and Thomas at once realized what a splendid challenge they
offered. He began making a series of long-distance moorland
walks.

In 1918, with his companion, Norman Begg, he repeated the
51 miles Colne to Doveholes walk first done by Cecil Dawson
in 1904. His time was 17 hours 59 minutes. He followed this by
a new walk, the 37½ miles circuit of the Derwent Watershed
which he completed in 11 hours 39 minutes. The watershed
embraces a horseshoe of extremely difficult moorland, including Kinder Scout and Bleaklow, and will always be one of the
hardest of the long-distance walks for which the Peak District
is famous.

A year later Thomas directed his attention to Wales where he
made the first traverse of the fourteen 3,000-ft. summits, now
one of the most popular long-distance walks in Britain.

It was in this same year—1919—that Thomas made his first
bid for that most coveted of long-distance walks, the Lake District Fell Record, then held by Dr. Wakefield. He discovered,
however, that strength and courage were in themselves not
sufficient for this difficult prize and he failed to gain the record.
Undeterred, Thomas carefully analysed his mistakes and re-
vised his strategy ready for the following year.

Paced by Wakefield himself, Thomas dinted the record a
little in 1920 by covering the same distance as his predecessor,
59 miles with 23,500 feet of ascent, in a shorter time. This was
not sufficient to make him the undisputed record holder, so two
years later he made a third and successful attempt. He covered
66½ miles and 25,500 feet of ascent within the time limit of
twenty-four hours—and he actually continued for another four
and a half hours, though this did not count towards the record.

Having accomplished the most difficult walks in England
and Wales, Thomas then turned to see what Scotland had to
offer. During the Whitsun of 1924 he made the first traverse of
all the 4,000-ft. summits, taking twenty hours, though of course
he used a car between Fort William and the Cairngorms, which

is no longer allowed by the modern rules. Unfortunately, the gilt was taken from the gingerbread by a rival group from the Fell and Rock Climbing Club who managed to do it in two hours less.

Though Thomas would have been the first to give credit to his companions on these marathon walks the fact remains that he was the one who really gave shape and standards to modern mountain walking.

A record such as this, compiled relatively late in life—he was 55 when he did the Scottish walk—would have satisfied most men. Thomas, however, was never one for retirement and he once remarked that the walks were nothing more than a useful, if somewhat novel, preparation for the Alps.

He had visited the Alps many times during his younger days, but it was not until 1923 that he had what he called his first 'serious season'. For five strenuous weeks he romped through the Diablerets, Mont Blanc area, Oberland and Valais, aided and abetted by his two guides, Joseph Knubel and Alexander Lagger. It was an impressive performance of stamina: twenty-four major summits, with the Charmoz, Grépon and Blaitière done in a single day and likewise the Jungfrau, Mönch and Gross Fiescherhorn. In three days they traversed the Zinal Rothorn, Dent Blanche and Matterhorn from Zinal to Zermatt.

When he returned the following year Knubel suggested that they should concentrate on peaks of 4,000 metres or more and treat anything smaller as incidentals or things to be done on an off day. Such an idea had an immediate appeal to Thomas— here was a target to aim at—the conquest of all the 4,000-metre peaks in the Alps!

It took him six years. The grand total was eighty-three peaks over 4,000 metres and thirty lesser summits. This averages nineteen peaks a year, which is an outstanding record for any-one, let alone a man who is approaching his sixtieth birthday.

He became the first Englishman to complete all the Alpine giants, and it is doubtful if it has ever been repeated.

No sooner had he completed his task, however, when friends began to get out their large-scale maps and point out isolated pinnacles which though not summits in themselves nevertheless topped the magic 4,000 metres. Thomas willingly took up any such challenges and perhaps his finest feat was the traverse of the Aiguilles du Diable on Mont Blanc du Tacul in 1932, only four years after the first ascent.

Any kind of adventure appealed to Thomas. When in his sixties, he was attracted to gliding and before long he had gained the triple record for height, endurance and distance. This mastered, he took up powered flight and celebrated his seventieth birthday by flying his Percival to Egypt.

On his return home the Second World War broke out and the R.A.F. requisitioned his plane. Feeling that they must be hard up to take his little Percival, Thomas bought them a Spitfire as well.

This indomitable man never seemed to tire. Even after the war he would roam the world, choosing the most unlikely routes in the hope of seeing something new or unusual. He died in October 1960, in his ninety-second year.

GEOFFREY WINTHROP YOUNG

(1876 – 1958)

WHEN MUMMERY VANISHED amidst the snows of Nanga Parbat in 1895 he left a vacuum in British mountaineering which seemed impossible to fill. Collie, Slingsby and others were still active, but their best Alpine work was done and it looked as though the most enterprising young men were turning more to British rock-climbing or the exploration of the distant Himalaya. Were the Alps finished as a field for endeavour?

Two men gave the answer. As the new century dawned the names of Ryan and Young began to be mentioned in connection with climbs harder than anything done before.

V. J. E. Ryan was a fascinating character if only because we know so little about him. He was reputed to be a difficult man to get along with—'not a very nice person', was how one of his contemporaries summed him up—and he shares with Mummery the distinction of being blackballed out of the Alpine Club. Nevertheless, he was a very good climber with two very good guides—the Lochmatter brothers—as his constant companions. The routes he made were regarded as too difficult in their day and it is only fairly recently that they have become popular.

Young, who was Ryan's great contemporary and often climbed with him, was an altogether different sort of person. He was always amongst the leaders of Alpine thought, always popular, and by his leadership and personality he rose to a position of great influence in British mountaineering.

Geoffrey Winthrop Young was born in 1876, the second son of Sir George Young of Cookham. Educated at Marlborough and Trinity he later studied abroad before becoming an assistant master at Eton where he stayed until 1905. From then until the War he was an Inspector of Schools for the Board of Education.

His father had played a small part in the early pioneering
days of climbing. In 1865 he had taken part in the first ascent
of the Jungfrau from the Wengen Alp, but during the following
season whilst descending Mont Blanc with two of his brothers
there had been an accident and one brother was killed. Sir
George immediately gave up the sport and the subject of
mountaineering was never allowed to be mentioned in his house
ever after.

Of course, in those days, mountaineering meant the Alps, not
Wales, and Sir George frequently took his family on walking
tours in the Principality. It was an introduction to the hills
which stirred the imagination of his second son and laid the
foundation for his future career. He also acquired that love of
Wales which was to remain all his life.

But already his mind was on more ambitious things. In his
school hymnal he scribbled 'Will I ever see the Alps?'

At Cambridge he went on reading parties to the Lake District where he first learned to climb steep rocks and he soon
became a leading member of the University night climbers—
young men who climb the college spires and pinnacles at night,
when (they hope) the authorities are asleep. Under a pseud-
onym Young published his *Guide to the Roofs of Trinity*.

His first visit to the Alps was in 1897 when he visited the
little known Tarentaise region, but in the following two seasons
he went to the Valais and the Oberland. With a group of Zinal
guides under the leadership of Louis Theytaz, he made the
third ascent of the Viereselsgrat on the Dent Blanche, always a
long and serious climb. He also made a number of daring solo
climbs, including the Grand Cornier, which he later ascribed
to the rashness of youth!

These introductory seasons proved beyond doubt that he was
a naturally gifted climber, very strong in wind and limb and
with an uncommon lack of fear. It was a combination of quali-
ties which was to place him in the forefront of Alpine climbing
during the next decade—that, and the fact that he discovered
a young guide called Josef Knubel who could match him step
for step.

Young's first great new route, however, was not made with Knubel but with that same Theytaz with whom he had climbed the Viereselsgrat. It was an ascent of the mighty Weisshorn from Zinal by a rib now called the Younggrat. Perhaps because of this success the Weisshorn always remained his favourite mountain and he later made two more new routes on the mountain.

But it was with Josef Knubel that he did his best climbs. They were an incredibly fit pair. On one occasion they climbed the Charmoz, Grépon and Blaitière in a single day because Young thought the three peaks made a geometric pattern which pleased him, and on another they traversed all the tops of Monte Rosa, followed by Lyskamm, Castor and Pollux, then back to Lyskamm, as a punishment for one of the other guides in the party whom Young thought was lazy! Despite such long expeditions, Young never had to spend a night in a forced bivouac.

Accompanied by Ryan, Young tried to climb the Furggen Ridge of the Matterhorn, possibly because this had been one of Mummery's great failures; but like Mummery, Young met with no success.

In the same year, 1905, and again with Ryan and the Loch-matters, he climbed the south-east face of the Weisshorn by a route which he straightened out the following season. It was a bold face climb which was not repeated until 1937, and it set the pattern of Young's great Pennine climbs—big, serious face-routes which few dared to follow. Only one climb proved an exception, the beautifully elegant Younggrat of the Breithorn which he did with Robertson and Mayor in 1906 and which has since become one of the classic climbs of the Zermatt area.

In 1906 he also climbed the south-west face of the Dom with Mayor and Gabriel Lochmatter, and the south-west face of the Täschhorn with Ryan and the Lochmatter brothers, Franz and Joseph.

Even by today's high standards the face of the Täschhorn is one of the most serious and difficult routes in the Alps. It is 900 metres high and subjected to stonefall. Young's party were fortunate in choosing a dry season but the ascent took them fifteen and threequarter hours, nine hours of which was spent on the final 300 metres. It was not repeated for twenty-nine years.

The crux was an overhang which the incomparable Franz Lochmatter overcame just when all seemed lost. Knubel, who was also present, called it a once-in-a-lifetime climb, and André Roch, who made the third ascent, said that though there were more difficult climbs there were none more treacherous or dangerous.

In the following year Young made the first direct ascent of the east face of the Zinal Rothorn, a climb similar to that on the Täschhorn, though not quite as desperate. The Rothorn climb has seldom been repeated because another and even finer way up the face was discovered later.

Meanwhile, Young was busily trying to revive the fortunes of the Climbers' Club at home, then at a low ebb. He began his gatherings at the little white inn at Pen y Pass to which he invited all manner of climbers and soon these Easter and Christmas meetings became a tradition. Families came along, too, and the whole affair had something of the party atmosphere with people climbing over the furniture showing off feats of strength. Everyone who was anyone in the world of British climbing came along, from the gentle Mallory to the fire-eating revolutionary Eckenstein.

In 1911 Young joined H. O. Jones for a season at Chamonix. They made a traverse of the Grandes Jorasses, making the first ascent of the west ridge and the first descent of the Hirondelles Ridge, which was not climbed until 1927. On a mountain like the Jorasses it was a considerable achievement and in recognition of it one of the many 'summits' of the mountain was christened the Pointe Young. On August 19 they made what was to prove Young's most popular climb—the Mer de Glace face of the Grépon. This was the climb which Mummery, Venetz and Burgener had tried and abandoned before they climbed the Grépon by its other face, above the Nantillons Glacier. Young's route is steep, on firm rock, and a great rock climb in the modern fashion.

Two other good climbs fell to Young before the Great War: L'Isolée of the Dames Anglaises and the Rote Zahn of the Gspaltenhorn.

When the war broke out, Young's convictions did not allow him to take part as a combatant. Instead he joined an ambulance unit and it was whilst he was serving with this on the Italian Front that he received a shattering blow which might easily have crushed a lesser man. An enemy shell took off his left leg below the knee.

How could a man with one leg climb mountains? Even as he lay on his hospital bed Young began to think of an answer. It might be impossible, but at least he intended to find out—what *was* impossible, was for him to give up the mountains altogether.

His first concern was for an artificial limb of appropriate design. Nothing that existed at that time could stand up to the sort of punishing treatment it would receive in rough mountain country, nor was there anything flexible enough for Young's purpose. He eventually designed his own model and got a friend to construct it in a workshop.

With it he spent many painful hours on the Welsh hills, perfecting the design and hardening the shattered stump of his own leg. Not until 1927 did he feel able to put it to its real test—the Alps.

In the three seasons 1927–29, Young climbed Monte Rosa, Wellenkuppe, Matterhorn, Petits Charmoz, Requin and Grépon. He made some climbs on the Zermatt climbers' 'nursery', the Riffelhorn, as well, but he found the Dolomites too steep for his artificial leg. Of course, he tried his favourite mountain, the Weisshorn, but unfortunately soft snow stopped him when he was only a few hundred feet from the summit.

Considerable publicity was given to these climbs—especially the Matterhorn ascent—in the expectation that Young's exploits would give fresh hope to the thousands of other ex-servicemen who had lost limbs in the war.

The end came in 1935 when he ascended the Zinal Rothorn with Josef Knubel, the first time they had climbed together since their great expeditions of pre-war days. On the ascent

LLIWEDD · The buttresses of Lliwedd presented the greatest challenge to the pioneers of Welsh climbing.
CLOGWYN DU'R ARDDU · Cloggy, the great modern cliff of Wales, exploited by Colin Kirkus and Edwards.

CRACKSTONE RIB, CARREG WASTAD · One of the most popular of
J. M. Edwards's climbs in the Llanberis Pass.

Young realized that he was not enjoying climbing any more and he there and then decided that this should be his last climb. The strain was proving too much—after all, he was nearing 60.

By an ironic twist of Fate he slipped on the way down and fell 80 feet, until Knubel held him superbly on the rope. A great climbing career had come to an end.

He had meanwhile become a lecturer in education at London University and a writer of no mean ability. In 1920 he published a textbook on climbing called *Mountain Craft* which was so comprehensive that it became the standard work for many years. This was followed seven years later by the first volume of his autobiography, *On High Hills*, in which he told the story of his early climbs with Knubel, a book which has become one of the classics of climbing literature. Not until 1951, however, did the sequel appear—*Mountains With A Difference*—telling of his remarkable fight back after the war. He also co-operated with Noyce and Sutton in *Snowdon Biography*, a history of climbing in Wales.

His poems, published earlier, were also popular and rank as some of the finest mountain poetry ever written. Nobody has ever quite managed to convey the same depth of feeling of the climber as Young did, and his poem, *The Cragsman*, has been re-printed in numerous anthologies.

Young was elected President of the Alpine Club in 1941 and despite the difficulties brought about by the war he threw all his influence into bringing about a governing body for climbing composed of representatives from all the clubs in the country. This became the British Mountaineering Council, which now speaks officially for British climbers at all national and international conferences wherever mountaineering interests may be involved. Young could foresee the need for this unified voice just as he foresaw the need for accurate guide-books to Welsh crags many years earlier.

In 1918 he had married Cecil Slingsby's daughter Eleanor and they had a son and a daughter. He died on September 8, 1958.

GEORGE LEIGH MALLORY

(1886 – 1924)

THE PRIORY WALLS were in a ruinous state, decayed and crumbling, with excellent hand and foot holds for any would-be climber. To the young boy from Winchester College they seemed a heaven-sent opportunity, allowing him practice for his forthcoming summer vacation in the Alps, where one of his tutors had promised to take him climbing. Since he had never even been on a mountain before a bit of practice might come in useful, he thought.

But the scramble on the old walls nearly proved his undoing. One of them crumbled beneath his weight and only a daring acrobatic leap saved him from serious injury. Had he been less of an athlete he would certainly have missed his summer climbing tour, perhaps never taken up climbing at all, and the world would not have heard of George Leigh Mallory.

Fate decided otherwise. In the entire history of mountaineering only a mere handful of men have become legends, and Mallory is one of them. Long after the names of more successful climbers have been forgotten, Mallory's name will be linked with Everest. He will be remembered not so much for what he did as what he was and what he symbolized. In many ways, he was born thirty years too late.

George Herbert Leigh Mallory was born in 1886 and brought up in Mobberley, Cheshire, where his father was rector. In 1900 he became a scholar at Winchester and came under the influence of a young tutor there, R. L. G. Irving, who was a keen Alpinist. Irving it was who took young Mallory on his first Alpine season in 1904—an event which was to influence his entire life.

He had already failed his entrance examination to the Royal Military Academy at Woolwich (without regret, it might be

added) and, undecided what he should do, he applied for an
exhibition to Magdalene College, Cambridge, where the Master
was A. C. Benson, a noted Alpinist. Much to everyone's surprise
Mallory got his scholarship, and there can be little doubt that
Benson favoured the application. As Irving dryly remarked, he
must have got the scholarship on the history he *promised* to read,
since he certainly had not read much before! However, he
graduated with honours in 1907 and became a master at
Charterhouse, where he remained until the 1921 Everest
Expedition, except for service in the artillery during the war.

He spent a second year with Irving in the Alps, but 1906
found him scrambling on the steep buttresses of Lliwedd in
Wales, pulling behind him a rope of undergraduate friends, who
trusted him implicitly, despite the fact he had never climbed on
British rock before. He took to it readily—one day he accidentally left a favourite pipe on a high ledge called the Bowling
Green, and had to make a new and difficult solo climb to
retrieve it.

This Welsh holiday was a turning point in his career not
only because he discovered the joys of rock-climbing, but also
because he met Geoffrey Winthrop Young.

It was the time when Young was reaching the height of his
great powers: a physical and intellectual dynamo who gathered
round him all that was best in British climbing. Mallory
quickly became a prominent member of Young's Pen y Pass
gatherings.

He made a striking personality in any company. In looks he
was as handsome as a film star, with large thoughtful eyes and
long lashes, 'like a Botticelli Madonna' one contemporary
wrote. He was so chivalrous that Young always called him Sir
Galahad and he seemed quite incapable of making enemies. In
the many words which were written about him and his exploits,
the outstanding tribute to his character lies in the fact that there
is not a single word of criticism.

His gentle and gentlemanly character could well have been
called softness or effeminacy by anyone who didn't know him.
In fact he was very tough and agile: he played both codes of

football for his college, rowed for it too, and was a first-rate gymnast.

Small wonder that he was idolized, one of those men who have greatness thrust upon them whether they want it or not. He himself would have claimed no more than that he was a member of a brilliant company of equals, but the fact remains that through no fault of his own, Mallory was always more equal than others.

In later years Young wrote that there were three outstanding climbers of those days: Pope, Herford and Mallory, and of these three Mallory was the greatest in unfulfilled achievement—so original and apart in his climbing that it never occurred to any-one to compare him with others or judge his performance by ordinary mountaineering standards.

He became the leading exponent of the open sort of climbing found on steep rock walls and slabs, as opposed to the older gully school of climbing. This suited his gymnastic ability and he climbed very fast.

The strange thing is that despite his fame and leadership his record of first ascents is very small, and hardly any of them are popular today. He made half a dozen new routes on Lliwedd and perhaps as many again on other Welsh crags. He went to 'look at' Clogwyn d'ur Arddu and he made the first ascent of the East Gully there, though he found the gaunt slabs and ver-tical walls of the rest of the cliff too difficult. It was seven years before anyone else made a climb there.

His climbing was by no means confined to Wales. He was with Young on the first ascent of the Carn Les Boel ridge in Cornwall, and he went to Skye where he made a route called Mallory's Slab, and where he took part with Shadbolt and Pye in the first ascent of the famous Crack of Doom.

With Young too he climbed in the Alps, though not on any of the former's big Alpine expeditions. They did the south-east ridge of the Nesthorn and the south ridge of the Unterbachhorn. Mallory also put up new variants on the Dent Blanche, Aiguille du Midi, and Charmoz. Mostly these were rock climbs, and it is as a rock-climber that he is remembered, though he always claimed that he preferred snow climbing above all else.

He married in 1914 and his wife bore him a son and two daughters. Both of the girls, Clare and Berridge, became well-known mountaineers.

Like his climbing, Mallory's writings were full of unfulfilled promise. Had he written more or lived longer, he might have become one of the best mountaineering authors. As it is he wrote only a few articles and part of a book about Everest. Two of his phrases have passed into climbing lore. In an article describing a climb on Mont Blanc he wrote:

Have we vanquished an enemy? None but ourselves. Have we gained success? That word means nothing here. . . . To struggle and to understand—never this last without the other; such is the law.

The other quotation has become a part of the English language and the most famous mountaineering sentence of all time:

'But why do you want to climb Mount Everest, Mr. Mallory?' asked a woman reporter.

'Because it is there,' he replied.

Mallory's life falls into two distinct phases, Everest and before Everest, the latter almost a preparatory period, an apprenticeship for the real job. Everest gripped him completely and he was in from the start in 1921.

Mallory was for three years the living soul of the offensive on Everest, wrote Norton, the leader of the 1924 Expedition. *I believe the thing was a personal matter with him, and was ultimately somewhat different from what it was to the rest of us.*

Of course the early expeditions were fumbling in the dark; nothing was known of the mountain, very little of the country. Even less was known about the effect of high altitudes on men and equipment.

Mallory flung himself into the struggle wholeheartedly, dominating everyone and everything—except the mountain. Mallory and Everest became synonymous.

Like all the pre-war expeditions the first one in 1921 was based in Tibet for the simple reason that it was politically accessible (though with a great deal of difficulty) whereas Nepal, on the southern side of the mountain, was closed to all foreigners. This made the northern approaches the only ones available and it was from the windswept North Col and on the bleak, slabby north face that the drama was played out.

On the initial expedition Mallory, with Bullock, was the first European to see the mighty north face and one of the party which was first to reach the North Col. Ironically, too, on a reconnaiscence expedition he was the first man to peer over a ridge into the Western Cwm on the Nepalese side—the cwm which was to be the key to the first ascent of the mountain in 1953. Mallory considered it impracticable.

On May 21 of the following year, Mallory, Morshead, Somervell and Norton made the first of many attempts to reach the top of Everest. It was destined to fail because their camp was too low, and it would have ended in disaster had not Mallory belayed the party with his axe when the others slipped. As it was the expedition ended in tragedy when seven porters were over-whelmed by an avalanche. Others, Mallory amongst them, barely escaped with their lives.

In 1924 came his third and final attempt to get to the top. Bad weather, sickness and accident dogged the party through-out but at last the plan of attack got under way. It was Mallory's plan and he meant it to succeed. . . .

It is almost unthinkable with this plan that I shan't get to the top, he wrote, *I can't see myself coming down defeated.*

Against Norton's advice he chose as his partner young Sandy Irvine, 22, an Oxford Rowing Blue and a man of magnificent physique. Unfortunately, Irvine had little climbing experience, but this did not seem to bother Mallory. 'We will stamp to the top with the wind in our teeth,' Mallory told him.

On June 8, 1924, they set out from Camp VI to climb the 2,000 feet which separated them from the roof of the world. Odell, who was moving up in support from Camp V caught a glimpse of them as they negotiated the first great step of the north ridge, then the weather closed in and they disappeared from view.

They were never seen again.

SIEGFRIED HERFORD

(1891 – 1916)

ENGLISH ROCK-CLIMBING began quite independently in two distinct ways. On the one hand there were the pioneers of the Lake District scrambling about on steep crags at Christmas and Easter as an exercise in home-made Alpinism, and on the other there was Fred Puttrell enjoying the dirty, small, but exceedingly steep gritstone of Wharncliffe near Sheffield. Each gave rise to a branch of the sport.

At first the mountain men dictated the course of events as people like O. G. Jones and Archer Thomson brought standards to the Lakes and Wales, but after the turn of the century the gritstoners took a hand and the fusing of the two breeds led to spectacular advances. Puttrell himself led the Ben Nuis Chimney in Arran, a very severe climb which was not repeated for over fifty years, and Fred Bottcrill, from Ilkley Moor, led the famous Botterill's Slab on Scafell, solo and carrying an ice axe —which he unfortunately dropped. These were certain pointers, though isolated. The real break-through came in the shape of a small curly-haired Welsh lad, trained on gritstone and destined to make his reputation in the Lake District.

Siegfried Wedgwood Herford was born in Aberystwyth in 1891. His first recorded climbs were done on the Gross Glockner in Austria when he was 16 years old, but it seems unlikely that he should not have tried his homeland hills before that time. Certainly he did some climbs on his return home, though when Laycock first met him on Kinder in 1910, the young Herford was still a novice.

He had become an undergraduate at Manchester University and so the moors and the steep little gritstone crags of the High Peak were readily accessible to him. His meeting with Laycock, who probably knew as much about gritstone climbing as

anybody at that time, was extremely fortunate and it placed
Herford on the path which many a climber has since followed:
an apprenticeship on the outcrops. With companions like
Laycock, Jeffcoat and A. R. Thomson he was soon mastering
the most difficult climbs of the day.

His favourite gritstone crag was Castle Naze, near to New
Mills and handy from Manchester. It is a small outcrop with
mostly easy climbs, but Herford used it in a way not seen before
—he climbed *across* the rocks instead of just *up* them. Of course,
this made a much longer climb, and it became known as a
girdle traverse. Nowadays there are very few climbing cliffs
which do not have at least one 'girdle'.

On the high windswept crags of Kinder itself he put up some
severe climbs such as Pagoda and Mermaid's Ridge, and at the
Roches he and his friends made the ever popular Jeffcoat's
Chimney. In 1913 Laycock published a book about outcrop
climbing called *Some Gritstone Climbs* which he dedicated to
Herford.

Meanwhile Herford was extending his experience beyond the
confining limits of gritstone. He tried limestone, and with
Thomson he made the first ascent of Ilam Rock in Dovedale,
encountering on it all the looseness and vegetation which
modern climbers take for granted but which was then held to
be unjustifiably dangerous. Though others followed him at
intervals, Thomson's account of the dangers of Ilam Rock did
much to discourage limestone climbing for many years.

In 1912 Herford visited Skye with Laycock and he also went
to the Dolomites with a new-found companion, G. S. Sansom,
with whom he was destined to do his greatest climbs. Together
these two paid several visits to Wasdale in connection with a
proposed guide-book to Scafell and they made the second ascent
of Botterill's Slab, the second ascent of Jones's Direct Route
from the Rake, the first Girdle Traverse of the crag, and they
finished off a route started by the Hopkinsons years ago and now
called Hopkinson's Gully.

The event of the season, however, was undoubtedly the
reaching of Hopkinson's Cairn on the Pinnacle Face of Scafell.

The cairn had been erected by Edward Hopkinson when he and his brothers had tried to descend the Pinnacle in 1887, and ever since that time climbers had been trying to find a route leading up to it. Now Herford solved the problem. On April 12, 1912, climbing in stockinged feet, he ran out 130 feet of rope in a single pitch and reached the cairn. It was an extraordinary performance and the key to the climb became known as Herford's Slab, an exposed and delicate pitch. Nowadays it can be done in a much safer way using modern techniques, but this only emphasizes what a daring lead Herford made.

During the same season Herford and Sansom first looked at the Central Buttress and wondered whether a way could be found up its towering bulk. They began by exploring out of Moss Ghyll, climbing round a corner, and coming across a large grass ledge now called the Oval. They were amazed to see a huge flake of rock soaring up above their heads like an inverted scimitar and seemingly detached from the parent buttress. As a way up it seemed quite hopeless, so they turned their attention to the big grooves which flank Moss Ghyll on that side and which were later to form another fine climb, Moss Ghyll Grooves, done by Kelly. Sansom made some progress up the grooves but eventually they gave up and went to climb on the nearby Pisgah Buttress instead.

The following June saw them both on the Oval again, this time determined to examine the Great Flake more closely. They observed that the first part, a sort of cracked bulging wall, was comparatively easy, but thereafter the Flake reared up for fully forty feet and overhung about twelve feet. Sansom led up the preliminary section but declined to tackle the Flake. Herford took Sansom's place, studied the problem, and declared it unjustifiable.

Sansom went abroad for the rest of the summer, but during his absence Herford took another look at the Flake, accompanied by his old friend Jeffcoat. From the top of another climb over on the left they traversed across, on to the Central Buttress, to a wide and comfortable stance now called Jeffcoat's Ledge. Here Jeffcoat belayed himself whilst his leader continued to

5*

traverse along the ever narrowing ledge which eventually
became a mere knife-edge and proved to be the top of the Great
Flake. In all his experience Herford had seen nothing like it
before: the huge flake was semi-detached from the rock so that
it was possible, though painful it was so sharp, to sit astride it.
The exposure was sensational.

Still belayed by the patient Jeffcoat, Herford descended the
Flake Crack to the Oval, though he had a bit of difficulty
through the rope jamming. Herford was now convinced that
the Flake could be climbed.

On April 19, 1914, Herford, Sansom, Gibson and Holland
made the first full-scale attempt on Scafell's Central Buttress.
Gibson was placed on top of the Great Flake and he lowered a
rope to Sansom, who, climbing in stockinged feet, managed to
struggle to the top. Next, Herford had a go and managed it
without any pull from the rope. Thus encouraged the three men
on top of the Flake descended by the easy Broad Stand route to
rejoin Holland who was still patiently waiting on the Oval.

Now that every possible exploration of the route had been
made, the time had arrived to lead it clean. Quite obviously, it
was going to be a desperate affair, but they had given considerable thought as to tactics. Consequently Sansom and Herford
climbed the introductory section and with Herford steadying
the leader's feet Sansom struggled up to the overhang, where
there is a conspicuously useful chock-stone jammed in the crack.
Sansom threaded a rope round this, passed his own rope
through the loop so formed and then descended to hand over
the lead to Herford.

Protected by the rope above him Herford made two attempts
to climb the overhanging part of the Flake, but failed. Then
Sansom tried, but he too failed. Neither Gibson nor Holland
wished to make an attempt so the route was abandoned for the
day, leaving the threaded rope in position. Poor Holland had
spent seven hours on the Oval.

Next day the rope loop, which was showing signs of wear,
was replaced and *two* climbing ropes threaded through it.
Sansom, tied on one rope, went up to the loop and hung on to

it whilst Herford, on the other rope, climbed up until he could use his companion's shoulder for his feet. As Herford moved up a little so Sansom moved up too until he was able to grasp the top of the chockstone. Once more using his friend as a foothold Herford managed to clamber over the overhang and before long reached the top of the Flake, much to everyone's relief!

One by one the rest of the party followed up the Crack, and they even invited a spectator to come along as last man—D. G. Murray, who later made the difficult Murray's Route on Dow Crag.

Feeling that they had done enough for one day the party traversed off from the top of the Flake. They completed the delicate upper part of the Buttress two days later, with Sansom leading. Their only regret was that Jeffcoat had not been present to take part.

The Central Buttress of Scafell—'C.B.' as it is affectionately known to all climbers—was regarded for many years as the hardest climb in Britain and even today, more than fifty years after the first ascent, it remains one of the great climbs in the country. Who knows what might have followed had the First World War not intervened?

Herford was no stranger to Wales, of course, where he was a member of Winthrop Young's Pen y Pass group. He went to the Alps with Young soon after making the Central Buttress ascent, and together they made several new and difficult climbs—little realizing that it would be the last time for either of them.

Like a good many of the younger generation Herford abhorred killing, even when disguised as war, so he answered the call of duty first as a War Correspondent, then an ambulance driver. But the horrors of the trenches bit into his soul until he became convinced that only by crushing Germany could the terrible slaughter of the Western Front be ended. He joined the famous Sportsmen's Battalion of the Royal Fusiliers.

Then, one day in 1916, whilst walking down a trench at Ypres, he carelessly exposed himself to a German sniper. Not yet 24 years old, the incomparable Siegfried Herford was dead.

HANS LAUPER

(1895 – 1936)

THE TREMENDOUS PUBLICITY which has been accorded in
recent years to the north face of the Eiger, has been directed at
the famous route via the White Spider, first done by Heinrich
Harrer in 1938. It is possibly the most difficult and dangerous
climb in the Alps, and the attempts on it have tended to over-
shadow the fact that the great face had an earlier and safer
ascent. Six years before Harrer's success, a Swiss mountaineer
called Hans Lauper made the first ascent of this most difficult
of north walls.

Lauper was something of an enigma. His ideals and thoughts
about climbing were in many ways Victorian, and yet it was he
who first seriously attacked the big north walls of the Western
Alps.

Born in Berne in 1895, Lauper had a brilliant academic
record at the university there, but once he had graduated he
seemed unsure about his future career. At first he tried Latin
scholarship, then, to be nearer the mountains, he became a
topographer, and finally, by complete contrast, a dentist. For a
short time he emigrated to the United States, but his love for
the Alps was too strong and he soon returned to settle in Zurich.

His mountaineering began in boyhood in his native Bernese
Alps, and though he later climbed in other regions of the Alps,
it was always the Oberland which held his special affection. He
knew it intimately, probably better than any man before or
since, and he was a natural choice as chief contributor when the
Swiss Alpine Club compiled their guide-book to the region.

The Bernese Oberland is a region where long climbs of a
mixed snow and rock character predominate and it was this
sort of background which determined the pattern of Lauper's
career, for he always went for the bigger peaks. Technical rock-

climbing did not greatly interest him—he never, for example, visited the Dolomites. His goal was one to which many climbers aspire but so few attain—an all round competence of a very high standard. That he succeeded is shown by his record which includes eighteen first ascents, all difficult, between 1915 and 1932. Amongst them were the north faces of the Stockhorn, Kamm, Mönch, Jungfrau and Eiger.

He climbed at a time when young continentals, especially from Austria and Germany, were flinging themselves desperately and often hopelessly at all sorts of difficult climbs. Lauper ignored the trend and remained a firm traditionalist. Whilst others froze to death in hastily contrived bivouacs, he would execute his meticulous plans in a single day.

This all round ability came from his attendance to the smallest points of technique, and superb fitness. He climbed like an automaton, with never a pause or hitch, but the slow steady rhythm such as guides employ. No holds ever came away in his hands, despite the rotten nature of some of the Oberland rock, and it is said that he never kicked down a single loose stone. He even managed to cross difficult glaciers without once letting the rope touch the ice, which is the ideal way of doing it, but seldom achieved in practice. In themselves these are only small points, but they show how thorough Lauper was in his climbing.

He was not what one might call a forceful personality. His temperament was calm, placid even, and sometimes strangers found him dull company though he could be gay enough with friends he knew well. The truth of the matter was that all his life he was suffering from the after effects of a boyhood operation, which in the end was suddenly to kill him.

His great routes were only attempted after long preparation. He would reconnoitre and photograph the proposed climb from every angle, sometimes taking years over the task—his Eiger route, for example, began as an idea in 1923 but was not realized until 1932.

The north face of the Eiger is divided into two parts by a big spur of the mountain. On the right of this spur, as one faces the mountain, is the vast concave triangle known as the Eigerwand

and the scene of Harrer's dramatic climb. On the left are steep slopes of ice, and rock walls descending from the Mittelegi Ridge. It was these slopes, and the dividing spur, which Lauper decided to attack.

On Saturday, August 20, 1932, Lauper with Alfred Zurcher and the guides Joseph Knubel and Alexander Graven, left the Kleine Scheidegg at 1.50 a.m. and followed the track of the mountain railway for fifteen minutes towards Grindelwald before striking off to the east over meadows and scree towards the foot of the Eigerwand. As they tramped along in the cold darkness they could see the lights of the Eigerwand Station of the Jungfrau railway, winking grotesquely high above them.

At 3.40 a.m. they put on the rope and attacked the first of the many rock steps which are such a feature of the route. Graven and Lauper led the way followed by Knubel and Zurcher.

They continued to traverse east, over the little Hoheneiss Glacier and some loose rocks until they were immediately below the Mittelegi Hut, then they turned to climb in a diagonal line upwards and slightly west, making for the great spur. Hardly had they started this, however, when there came the warning rattle of stones from above, probably caused by parties starting out to climb the Mittelegi Ridge. They shouted warnings, and the stones ceased—it was the only stonefall they encountered on the entire expedition.

By 6 a.m. they had arrived at a remarkable ledge which gave them views of the big rock buttress they had to ascend in order to reach the upper part of the face. Lauper had feared that this buttress might prove unclimbable, but they were delighted to discover that it was split by a deep crack. The crack was difficult but they managed to climb it by 8.36 a.m. It was the key to the upper face.

After thirty minutes' rest they began a steep snow climb, first straight up and then in a long traverse to the right to gain the northern spur. It was one of the most trying parts of the entire climb, for the snow was extraordinarily steep and there was no hope of stopping a slip if one occurred. 'We are all of us a bit crazy,' remarked Knubel with grim humour.

At last, about noon, the long traverse was completed and they found a good resting place where they could catch up on their appetites. There was a thousand feet of climbing still to be done, and it was to prove much harder than they expected.

At first good snow slopes helped them to make rapid progress, but when these ended abruptly against a wall of rock the climbing became more serious. Graven led up the rock and then, leaving Lauper below, called for the second pair to climb. In this way Zurcher and Knubel could use Graven's rope as extra handhold and so overcome the problem more quickly. Finally, after what seemed an eternity, Lauper joined his leader.

They were now nearing the summit ridge, but the Eiger was not finished with them yet. A final outcrop of rock, horribly loose, had to be climbed by means of an ice-filled overhanging crack. Graven led it, fighting the whole way, for it turned out to be Grade VI—the hardest standard of rock-climbing. It proved to be the crux. Much to their relief only a gentle snow slope remained to the summit, which they reached about 4 p.m.

There will never be any question of Lauper's Route ousting Harrer's in popularity, if only because the latter takes a more direct, though more dangerous, route to the top. In difficulty they are said to be equal, though there can be few climbers who have done both of these very serious routes. Quite recently there has been another and even more difficult climb done on the face—the Harlin Route, named after the American climber who was killed on the first ascent, but Lauper's will always be the safest way up this grim battleground.

Hans Lauper set a standard for north wall climbing which his successors, for good or ill, chose to ignore. With more efficient equipment and clothing it has been proved possible to stay out on the mountains even in severe blizzards for days on end. The calculated, swift decisive thrusts of men like Lauper have been replaced by siege tactics.

Hans Lauper died suddenly in Zürich in 1936. He was just 40 years old.

FRANCIS SYDNEY SMYTHE

(1900 – 1949)

OF ALL THE British climbers who were active between the two World Wars, Frank Smythe was probably the one best known to the general public. His books were very popular because he had a way of explaining climbing in terms which even a layman could understand and he injected into them something of the emotions of the mountaineer. Smythe was probably as responsible as anyone for the post-war surge of interest in climbing.

He was born in 1900, a somewhat frail child who was considered delicate because of a persistent heart 'murmur'. This affected his early education and when he went to Berkhamstead School he was somewhat behind his age group in the traditional subjects and because of his supposedly frail condition he was not allowed to play games. There thus existed a double gulf between himself and his contemporaries and he remembered his schooldays with bitterness in later life.

In fact, he never quite got over this upbringing which left him with a nagging inferiority complex all his life. He liked best to be alone in the hills, or with one or two chosen companions, though he could be a valuable member of a team as he demonstrated on the Everest Expeditions.

From school he went to Faraday House Engineering College and then spent two years in Austria studying for his profession. Here he became passionately fond of mountains and climbing, though he had done a little before at home. Later he returned to Austria on a holiday with Campbell Secord and wrote of their experiences in *Over Tyrolese Hills*, one of the most relaxing mountaineering books ever written and a good introduction to the Tyrolean mountains.

He went to South America as a trained engineer, disliked

the job, so came home and joined the R.A.F. In 1927 he was invalided out, and from then on devoted his whole time to mountaineering and writing.

This was the year in which he sprang to prominence in the Alpine world. After an early start to the season, spent in Corsica and the Mont Blanc group, he returned home for a short time, then went out again in July. He teamed up with J. H. B. Bell and together they repeated the Ryan-Lochmatter route on the Aiguille du Plan—the first time it had been climbed since Ryan's ascent twenty-one years previously! Then, with Graham Macphee, Smythe made a sensational bad weather traverse of the Aiguille Blanche de Peuterey, always one of the most difficult of the Mont Blanc satellites.

In the following month he joined Graham Brown, and on September 1 and 2 they made a new major climb on the Brenva Face. They called it the Sentinelle Rouge from a big red pillar near its foot.

The principal feature of the Brenva Face at this point is a great couloir which makes any route dangerous because of avalanches. Climbers have to make sure that they are out of the couloir before the sun rises and the warmth-giving rays soften the snow slopes. Across this couloir, as they climbed the Sentinelle, Smythe and Brown could see an even finer route, but the season was too advanced for them to explore it.

They returned the following year, crossed the couloir again and climbed up a series of rock buttresses and ice ridges. The going was even more difficult than that of the previous year but at last they won through to the summit of Mont Blanc. They called their climb Route Major, and along with the Sentinelle Rouge, it was the finest inter-war achievement of any British guideless party in the Alps. Five years later Graham Brown returned to the Brenva Face and made yet a third route —the Pear Buttress—which was even more difficult, but this was done with two guides, including Alexander Graven who the previous year had led the Lauper Route on the Eiger.

In 1930 Smythe joined Dyhrenfurth's International Kangchenjunga Expedition. The party was almost overwhelmed by an avalanche which killed one of the porters, and they did not succeed in climbing the mountain, but Smythe became fascinated by the Himalaya.

He returned the following year with his own team to attempt Kamet (25,447 feet)—the highest mountain climbed at that time and the first over 25,000 feet. It was a double success because Smythe, Shipton, Holdsworth and the porter Lewa reached the top on June 21 and two days later Greene, Birnie and Kesar Singh repeated the ascent. No fewer than eight previous expeditions had attempted the mountain and Smythe's success was a triumph of meticulous organization.

With such experience behind him Smythe was a natural choice for the 1933 Everest Expedition, when he equalled the altitude record set up by Norton in 1924—28,126 feet. He also showed superb icemanship: 'Without Frank we should never have reached the North Col,' one of his colleagues said later.

Of course, the expedition did not climb Everest nor did the two later expeditions of 1936 and 1938 which Smythe accompanied. In the meantime, he climbed in the Garhwal Himalaya and the Canadian Rockies until the Second World War broke out and he was given the job of training troops in mountain warfare.

But it was his books above all which meant most to the man in the street. He wrote or edited some twenty-seven of them, which is a prodigious output by any standard and quite phenomenal in such a specialized subject as mountaineering. Many of the books consisted almost entirely of photographs, and Smythe was a superb mountain photographer with a great eye for texture—his snow scenes are extremely beautiful.

In 1949 Smythe went to India to organize a new expedition comprising only himself and his Sherpas. Suddenly, he was struck by food poisoning and malaria, and though he was flown home for treatment he suffered a relapse from which he never recovered.

COLIN KIRKUS

(1910 – 1940)

THE MOTOR CYCLE roared north from Kendal, over the summit of Shap and on towards Scotland and Ben Nevis. Crouched over the handlebars was the bespectacled figure of Maurice Linnell and behind him, almost lost in a mountain of camping gear, Colin Kirkus. It was the Easter of 1934, and in the previous three years or so these two young men had shot like brilliant meteors across the British climbing scene. As the snow-clad Highlands opened up before them it seemed as though the motor-bike was carrying them into a glorious future.

Seven years before, young Colin Kirkus had persuaded his parents to take a family holiday at Bettws y Coed. Usually they holidayed on the Welsh coast, but Colin was keen to get to grips with mountains and he had had his imagination stirred by reading George Abraham's *British Mountain Climbs*. He wanted to be nearer the heart of things, but his parents were reluctant to stay in the bleak surroundings of the Ogwen Valley. Bettws y Coed was a compromise.

He had nobody to climb with but this did not stop him from setting off for Craig yr Ysfa, a lonely cliff in the Carneddau mountains, armed with a rope.

Craig yr Ysfa is split by numerous large gullies and it was to these that he directed his attention. First he climbed the simple Arch Gully, then he attempted B Gully and fell as he tried to struggle over a smooth overhanging chockstone. Fortunately, a large ledge prevented him from going too far, so picking himself up, he tried again. He fell once more. Ruefully deciding to give the mountain best, he went home.

Kirkus was born in Liverpool in 1910. He first went to Wales when he was 7 years old and right from the start there was something about the wild hills of the Principality which appealed to him. He scrambled and walked there whenever he could and by the age of 12 he was acting as 'guide' to his younger brothers.

His first real climbing, however, was during the Bettws y Coed holiday. Not content with near disaster on Craig yr Ysfa he tried his luck on the Holly Tree Wall at Cwm Idwal. The wall is very exposed since it overlooks a tremendous sweep of steeply tilted rock known as the Idwal Slabs, and Kirkus chose for his climb a route called Lazarus. It is in fact quite a difficult route and before long the young Kirkus was trapped, unable to move up or down. But he had with him his rope and this he used to lasso, cowboy fashion, a small bollard of rock. He swarmed up the rope and thankful to find the going easier, escaped.

Kirkus didn't seem to mind his lucky escape—already he possessed those nerves of steel which became the hallmark of his great ascents.

In the following year when he was 18, Kirkus joined the Climbers' Club. One of his contemporaries, who met him at Helyg, the club hut in Wales, described him as 'rather strange looking'. In fact he was a fairly ordinary-looking young man with slight build, of medium height, a longish face and a characteristic quiff of hair. He would eat anything that was going, and before long he had acquired a reputation as 'a gannet', and since rumours of his escapades had got round the Club, he was regarded as slightly crazy.

At the Helyg hut he met Alan Hargreaves, another climber with a reputation to keep up, so together they tried the difficult Holly Tree Wall in heavy nailed boots in the pouring rain. This was so successful that they formed a partnership, known to the other members as The Suicide Club. Nevertheless it was a fruitful partnership with Hargreaves transforming an untutored genius into a brilliant climber. Twice during this period Kirkus fell off, and was held by Hargreaves.

In between his visits to Wales Kirkus also visited Helsby Crag, a fine sandstone outcrop in the Wirral which has been popular with Liverpool climbers for many years. At that time men like Marshall, Hicks and Edwards climbed at Helsby and the standard of performance was very high, but when Marshall was killed on the crag whilst preparing notes for a guide-book, it was Kirkus who was asked to take over. With Hargreaves as partner he added nineteen new routes, most of a very high standard.

Strangely enough, Kirkus did not take to gritstone, but he did climb on the Cornish cliffs and one of his routes is the popular Pendulum Chimney on a cliff called Chair Ladder. The chimney got its name from a block which, though wedged in the chimney, rocks ominously.

It was inevitable that Kirkus should meet up with another Helsby tiger, F. E. Hicks, but as it happens the meeting took place quite accidentally at Helyg. Kirkus was alone, looking for a partner, but Hicks was a little wary of inviting him to join his own group because of Kirkus's reputation. Eventually, however, Hicks relented—and Kirkus promptly led Lot's Groove on Glyder Fach and Central Route on the Terrace Wall of Tryfan. Both were new climbs and extremely fierce—even Hicks could not follow on the Terrace Wall, and Kirkus had to finish it solo.

Three days later, with Hargreaves, Kirkus made the second ascent of Longland's Climb on Clogwyn d'ur Arddu. It took them four and a half hours, much of the time being spent in removing grass from the holds—'gardening', as climbers call it. It was scarcely a year since Longland had first led this very exposed climb on the forbidding precipices of Clogwyn d'ur Arddu, and it had the reputation of being one of the hardest climbs in Britain.

With the second ascent Kirkus ended his apprenticeship. Now he had proved himself a master, and the next three years were full of brilliance.

In 1930, with Graham Macphee, Kirkus led the Great Slab of Clogwyn d'ur Arddu, a major breakthrough on the cliff. Though nowadays it is regarded as one of the easier climbs, it was a great achievement on Kirkus's part for he had to climb through the barrier of overhangs which prevented access to the

West Buttress, and then run out more than 120 feet of rope before he could find a safe stance. Nowadays it is done differently, and the rock is clean, but Kirkus was climbing new ground, loose and vegetated. It is doubtful if there existed at that time another climber who combined sufficient nerve and skill to do what Kirkus did.

It was after this climb that the name Cloggy was coined for Clogwyn d'ur Arddu; a name which has stuck ever since, much to the annoyance of ardent Welshmen.

Turning his attention to the Lake District Kirkus looked at the black forbidding East Buttress of Scafell, a sombre cliff over the other side of Mickledore from Central Buttress and the other famous routes. The result of his investigations was Mickledore Grooves, the first breech in the crag. In one season Kirkus had demonstrated the possibilities of the two cliffs—Cloggy and the East Buttress—which were to dominate the post-war years of British climbing. They are still the two favourite playgrounds for the experts.

Before the year was out he had added his famous Direct Route on the sheer Nose of Dinas Mot in the Llanberis Pass, the top pitches of which took four to five hours and called forth the comment that a ladder would be needed by most people! Even by today's high standards none of these climbs is despised by experts—indeed for twenty years they represented the ultimate in British rock climbing.

Unlike his great contemporary, Edwards, who lived on the edge of his nerves, Colin Kirkus was a man who seemed to have no knowledge of fear. A friend once said that Kirkus could stand for hours on next to nothing, a hundred feet above his second man, with complete indifference. Though he was not really a strong man, he seemed to have complete confidence in his own ability, but like that other great climber, Owen Glynne Jones, he was ungainly to watch.

A comparison with Edwards is inevitable since they were the two great innovators of the 1930's. There were others who might match them in skill—Maurice Linnell, for example—but none had that vital spark which they possessed and which makes for greatness. Yet they had it differently—Edwards plugging away at the Three Cliffs and the Devil's Kitchen area and altering basic conceptions of the sport, Kirkus flitting like some glorious butterfly from cliff to cliff picking off the lines of greatness.

In 1931 he returned to Craig yr Ysfa, where he had started, and made a remarkable solo climb up the Pinnacle Wall. The Pinnacle Wall is an extremely steep and impressive piece of rock with a curious ledge running across it. Kirkus traversed on to the ledge, crossed it, then climbed the pinnacle itself and from there stepped on to a steep slab on the facing wall and so to the top. It is still graded as Hard Severe, even though it is now perfectly cleaned; nothing demonstrates more forcibly Kirkus's total absence of fear.

On Cloggy he put up Chimney Route, Pedestal Crack, Birthday Crack (on his birthday) and Curving Crack. As if to find somewhere fresh he also made a couple of new climbs on the somewhat remote Great Slab of Cwm Silyn.

He kept himself fit by cycling from Liverpool to Helyg and on occasions even walking it. There is no doubt that he thought he would be chosen for the 1933 Everest Expedition (though his Alpine record was undistinguished) and he might have been, too, but for influence in certain quarters. His failure to be chosen was a bitter disappointment, though he gained some consolation by going on Marco Pallis's Gangotri Expedition. He took a leading part in the ascent of Bhagirathi III (6,866 metres) a climb said to involve some of the hardest high altitude rock-climbing ever attempted.

And so to 1934 and that fateful Easter journey to Ben Nevis with Linnell. They camped below the mountain which was well covered with snow and on the Saturday set off to climb the Castle; one of the standard routes. They made good time and had reached the treacherous slabs just below the top when a snow step broke, and Linnell, who was leading, slid down the cliff. There was nothing Kirkus could do. Plucked from his own steps by Linnell's fall he tumbled after his leader, banging from rock to rock, hissing through now slopes. Linnell was killed outright, strangled by the rope. Kirkus was seriously injured, temporarily half-blinded.

Even in such dire straits his supreme calmness never deserted him. He anchored Linnell's body, carefully marking the place so that it could be easily recognized and then he dragged himself off the mountain all the weary miles to Fort William.

For Colin Kirkus it was the end of a brilliant climbing career. Though he recovered completely, the impetus of exploration had left him and he confined himself to modest climbs, frequently instructing beginners. He made a brief comeback to do the Glyder Fach guide-book, which showed he had lost none of his old nerve and skill, but he didn't keep it up. It was at this time that he wrote his delightful book for novices called *Let's Go Climbing*.

On the outbreak of war he joined the R.A.F. and became a navigator. In 1940 his plane disappeared on a bombing mission over Germany.

JOHN MENLOVE EDWARDS

(1910 – 1958)

THE STORY OF John Menlove Edwards is one of sheer dark tragedy. Here was a man gifted more than most in mental capacity and physical strength; a man who created some brilliant climbs and set the pattern for modern progress, yet one for whom life was nothing but a bitter twisted struggle.

He was born the youngest son of a country parson. Judged by the middle-class standards of the times the family were poor, though Edwards went to the usual public school and hated every minute of it. Early on in life he had the misfortune to see his father paralysed in one accident and his favourite brother killed in another and these tragedies may well have had a permanent effect on his young mind. He grew into a shy, introverted boy.

His family background was one of socialist Christianity which influenced Edwards in his choice of career as a medical missionary, but before he graduated he lost his Faith, and seeking to replace it with science he became a psychiatrist.

For one of his temperament this was not perhaps the wisest profession to choose and yet he was very successful at it, doing some good work in a clinic he ran. Unfortunately, his concern over the working of the human mind was so total that everything he did was subjected to rigorous analysis. In many respects he was his own chief patient.

Edwards cared nothing for the beauty of the hills or the niceties of technique—for him climbing was a physical and mental struggle, finding out just how far he could go. He once wrote a classic little essay called *A Great Effort* which poked gentle fun at those who wanted to know how great climbs were done, but which, at the same time, shows just how fully the author was aware of the mental struggle involved in climbing. To use a modern climbing phrase, Edwards 'pushed it' as far as he could—and not only on the hills. It led him into some other daring adventures such as swimming the raging cataracts of the Linn of Dee and trying to row across the storm-swept Minch.

It is important to understand this involvement which Edwards had with extreme limits, for then everything he did in the mountains falls into place.

He first came to prominence in 1931 when he climbed the Flake Crack of Scafell's Central Buttress in nailed boots instead of the traditional plimsolls, and showed at the same time that the awkward chockstone which caused Herford so much trouble could be overcome without aid from the second man. In the same year, with his fellow Liverpudlian, Kirkus, he made the first ascent of Chimney Route on Cloggy.

Shortly after this he began his probings of Clogwyn y Geifr, the repulsive-looking buttresses which surround the celebrated chasm of the Devil's Kitchen near Ogwen. There existed at that time only two climbs on these rocks, that of the Kitchen itself and the nearby Hanging Garden Gully. In August 1932 Edwards began his campaign with a solo ascent of Devil's Buttress, and then, between March and September of the following year he added fourteen more routes and a variant. A campaign like this was typical of Edwards' thoroughness, though in this particular instance none of the climbs became popular.

Clogwyn y Geifr was virtually unknown when Edwards started and it is a crag of unusually loose rock. These two factors paved the way to the two most notable aspects of his career: his guide-books and his pioneering of what was then regarded as bad rock.

His guide-book work came about as the result of a pre-war magazine called the *Mountaineering Journal*. When it first appeared in 1932 it promised its readers guides to all the hills of Britain and it began with an article on Holly Tree Wall and the East Wall at Cwm Idwal, written by J. M. Edwards. Then the

Climbers' Club took over responsibility for publishing Welsh guide-books and Edwards was a natural choice as a contributor. His first volume, *Cwm Idwal*, appeared in 1933.

The book was in several respects quite different from the already familiar guide-books to the Lakeland crags which H. M. Kelly was producing for the Fell and Rock Club. Instead of the matter-of-fact clinical style which Kelly employed, Edwards tried to place each climb in relation to the cliff as a whole, leaving much of the detail to the imagination of the climber. It gave the climber much more freedom in choosing how he should tackle a route or where he should belay and so forth, but it was a much wordier system than Kelly's. As routes grew numerous on the rocks so Edwards' system grew more unmanageable, and Kelly's method won the day in the end.

Nevertheless his guide-books will always be remembered because they are full of neat phrases. He was a master of what the Americans call the 'throw away line' based on British understatement. For example, the rather monotonous sweep of the Idwal Slabs he sums up by writing, *The climbing is much of the stepping-up type.* Of the extremely difficult routes on Cloggy he comments, *One would not advise a beginner to lead here too immediately.* His description of the loose rocks of Clogwyn y Geifr is classic:

It has every natural advantage, being steep, composed of pretty rocky sort of rock and being covered with vegetation: also parts of it have been long overdue for public exploitation. It is the sort of place where one can feel the full glory of stepping with perfect safety on somebody else's considered opinion. It is not, of course, the cliff for those who attack the problem tooth and nail nor yet for those who rise by seizing every opportunity, but I think it may now be considered safe for democracy. It is years since anybody was killed there.

The guide-book work necessarily concentrated Edwards' efforts on those cliffs to be covered. In the case of Tryfan he teamed up with a young expert called Wilf Noyce. Together they solved the 'last great problem' of Soap Gut, an evil looking groove on the Milestone Buttress which kept its reputation for difficulty for some years, but which is now considered fairly easy. They also made the second ascent of Munich Climb, removing the three pitons planted by the visiting German party, who made the first ascent in 1936.

On Lliwedd, again working for the guide-book, he made the first ascent of the Central Gully Direct—a difficult climb not often done even today.

His fondness for steep, loose, unexplored rock quickly led him to the short fierce cliffs of the Llanberis Pass: Dinas Cromlech, Carreg Wastad, and Clogwyn y Grochan. It was his pioneering of these cliffs which gives him a special place in mountaineering history because until Edwards began nobody had given them more than a casual glance.

Many of the popular climbs on these three cliffs were of Edwards' invention. They extend from Holly Buttress and Spiral Stairs which he did in 1931 through such favourites as Crackstone Rib and Hazel Groove in 1935, Brant and Slape in 1940 to the Central Gully of the Grochan in 1949. His was the first route to appear on each of the cliffs, and though some of them (but not all) seem fairly easy by modern standards it must be remembered that since they were first made they have had hundreds of ascents and are now clean and sound, where they were once vegetated and loose.

The climbs on the three cliffs were also exceedingly steep, and in this combination of steepness, looseness and vegetation Edwards was once again pushing the standards of what was acceptable. He created more than just a few climbs: he created a new outlook on climbing altogether.

Like his contemporaries Edwards climbed with hemp rope and nailed boots, though he cared very little for his equipment. His boots frequently went un-nailed when the originals fell out and he would undertake the most difficult climbs with casual acquaintances, including ill-equipped young novices.

Of his other climbs round Llanberis the choicest are Western Slabs on Dinas Mot and the magnificent Bow Shaped Slab on Cloggy, but he was not a one to wander very far from the road if he could help it.

Meanwhile his professional life was becoming increasingly frustrating to him. Like many good practical scientists he had dreams of making a major break-through in his chosen subject. He saw himself in the role of theoretician, so throwing up his job he shut himself away in a lonely Welsh cottage in order to commit his theories to paper. When the work was done it was rejected out of hand by his fellow psychiatrists as being totally incomprehensible. It was a blow from which he never recovered.

The rest of his story is almost inevitable. His brain began to give way to fantasies. He developed an increasing persecution mania which extended to his closest friends.

On February 27, 1958, John Menlove Edwards died from swallowing potassium cyanide.

EPILOGUE

THE START OF the Second World War seems a good time at which to close this account of some of the climbing pioneers. The men and women included in this book are of a distinct breed; a direct line of descendants, with each generation building on what their forefathers had achieved, yet without radically altering the whole. From start to finish there is an undeniable unity about them.

But even before the guns had started to rumble across Europe, cracks were beginning to appear in the mountaineering edifice. Gods were being pushed from their pedestals and sacred cows violently slaughtered.

A new ethos was emerging. To place a finger on an exact date and place would be impossible. Perhaps it even started with Mummery on the north face of the Plan, or Young on the Täschhorn, or Lammer and Lorria, or Blanchet and Mooser— or indeed, anyone who did anything out of the ordinary. Perhaps it did not consciously start at all, but like Topsy, just growed.

By popular tradition, however, the new spirit is thought to have started in the Eastern Alps, and certainly by the mid-1930's it was well established there. Fundamentally it was startling in its simplicity: *anything goes*.

Like all new movements it had fumbling beginnings, and since mountain climbing does not encourage mistakes, the beginnings were disastrous. Men died senselessly.

Going, as they did, against the mainstream of tradition, the new climbers could not help but invoke the wrath of the established authorities. 'Suicide', was one of the milder epithets used to describe such goings-on. Because they used pitons, they were contemptuously called 'engineers' and 'the dangle and whack boys', and since they mostly (but by no means all) came from the Eastern Alps they were referred to collectively as 'the

Munich School'. Seeking to explain the unorthodox methods of these climbers in rational terms, English mountaineers, properly shocked, attributed it to the rise of National Socialism.

It is easy now to sneer at the traditionalists, but there was some substance in their objections. The fanatical approach *was* cultivated by the Nazi and Fascist parties, to encourage inexperienced youths to try and copy the experts, and the movement *did* begin calamitously. Men died deliberately and coldly on the Eiger, and whole expeditions were practically wiped out on Nanga Parbat and Kangchenjunga. Hindsight is easy, foresight much more difficult.

The new movement found its earliest expression in attacks on the great *nordwands:* most significantly the successful attacks on the Matterhorn in 1931 and the Eiger in 1938. It was only after the war, however, that the new movement gained ground, enormously helped by the technological improvements of the age such as nylon rope and duvet clothing. Protection such as the pioneers never dreamt was possible is now accepted as commonplace and since protection inspires confidence, the leading climbers have pushed the limits to the extreme.

The technological and mental breakthroughs have combined to produce formidable results. All the great faces of the Alps have been climbed, many of them in winter as well as summer, and all the 8,000-metre peaks of the Himalaya have been conquered, some of them several times by different routes. Even Everest has been traversed.

So the war seems the logical place at which to draw the barrier. The new climbers are much more professional, in every honorable sense of the word, than their predecessors. They have to be—dedication by itself is no longer sufficient. Read for contrast Whymper's *Scrambles*, which deals with the great problem of 1865 and then Gillman and Haston's *Eiger Direct*, which deals with the great Alpine problem of a century later. Both Whymper and Haston are dedicated men—but the difference is still enormous.

Only one thing remains unchanged and that is the eternal challenge of the mountains. A hundred years ago when the last of the great Alpine peaks was conquered, climbers were saying that the sport was finished. In fact, it had scarcely begun, and despite the modern advances it still has a long way to go. The challenge stretches out, limitless and infinitely variable into the future.